B.C. REINVENTS THE WHEEL

BY MASTROIANNI AND HART

⊞ WILLOW CREEK PRESS®

Published by Willow Creek Press, Inc.
P.O. Box 147, Minocqua, Wisconsin 54548

Printed in China

FORWARD

When asked who influenced me when I created *Garfield*, I never fail to mention Johnny Hart and *B.C.* My bookshelves are crammed with dozens of yellowed and tattered *B.C.* paperbacks. *B.C.* just oozed with Johnny's wacky take on life and passion for all things silly and fun.

He taught me to relax and to just have fun with my comic strip. If you have fun doing a comic strip, people have fun reading it! ... Duh...

When I do a really silly strip, I always give Johnny a nod when I sign it...

And what better honor can a comic strip enjoy than to have it lovingly carried on by family. Mason and Mick Mastroianni have certainly inherited the Hart "silly" gene, for *B.C.* is just as funny as ever under their able pens.

I look forward to another lifetime of laughs from *B.C.*!

–Jim Davis (creator of *Garfield*)

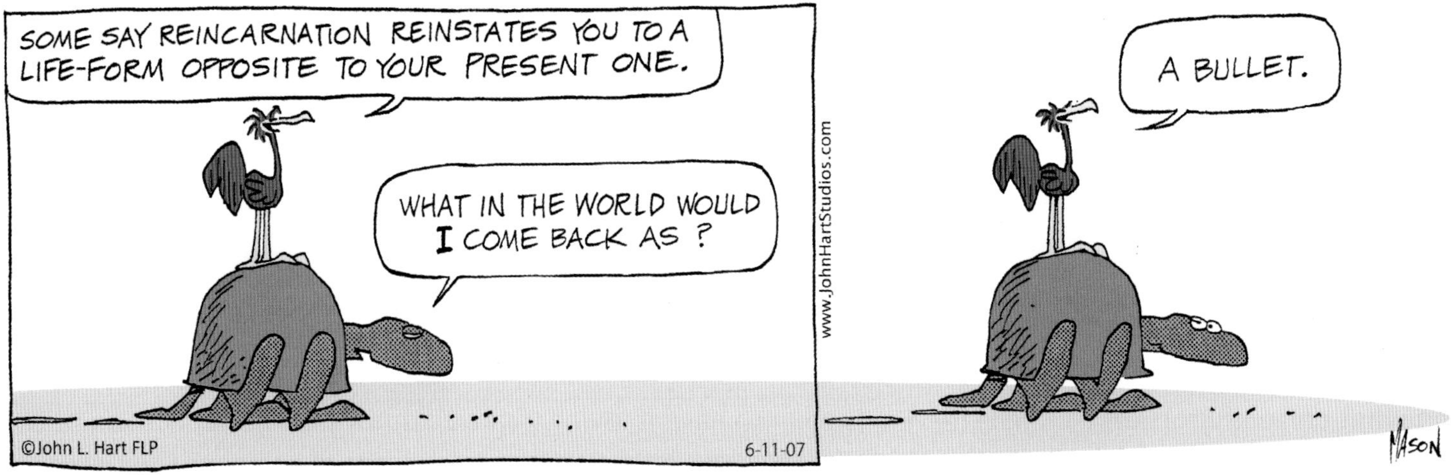
SOME SAY REINCARNATION REINSTATES YOU TO A LIFE-FORM OPPOSITE TO YOUR PRESENT ONE.
WHAT IN THE WORLD WOULD I COME BACK AS ?
A BULLET.
www.JohnHartStudios.com
©John L. Hart FLP
6-11-07
MASON

In April of 2007, when Mason Mastroianni flew from Minneapolis to Binghamton to attend his grandfather's funeral, little did he know how much his life was about to change. Mason's beloved "Pops" was none other than Johnny Hart, creator of the comic strips, *B.C.* and *Wizard of Id.*

In just two short months, Mason left an Emmy Award-winning position as a computer graphics animator, taught himself to draw the caveman characters, and became the new *B.C.* head-writer and cartoonist.

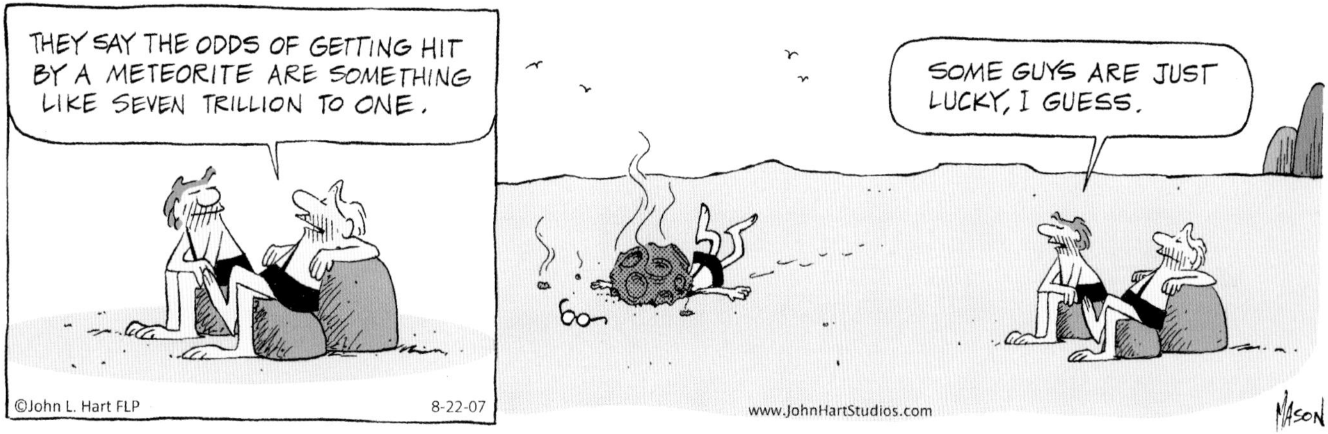
THEY SAY THE ODDS OF GETTING HIT BY A METEORITE ARE SOMETHING LIKE SEVEN TRILLION TO ONE.
SOME GUYS ARE JUST LUCKY, I GUESS.
©John L. Hart FLP
8-22-07
www.JohnHartStudios.com
MASON

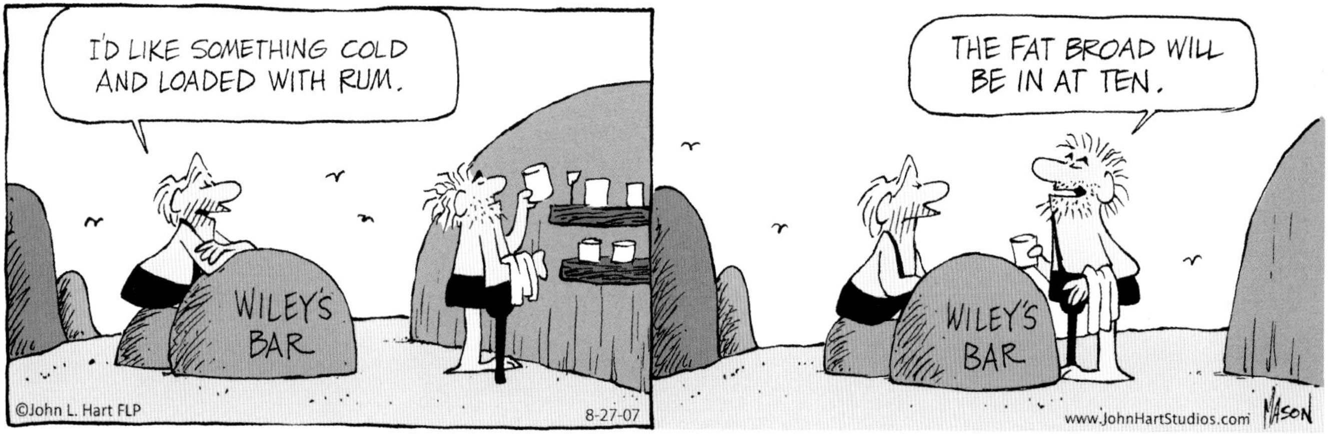
I'D LIKE SOMETHING COLD AND LOADED WITH RUM.
WILEY'S BAR
THE FAT BROAD WILL BE IN AT TEN.
WILEY'S BAR
©John L. Hart FLP
8-27-07
www.JohnHartStudios.com
MASON

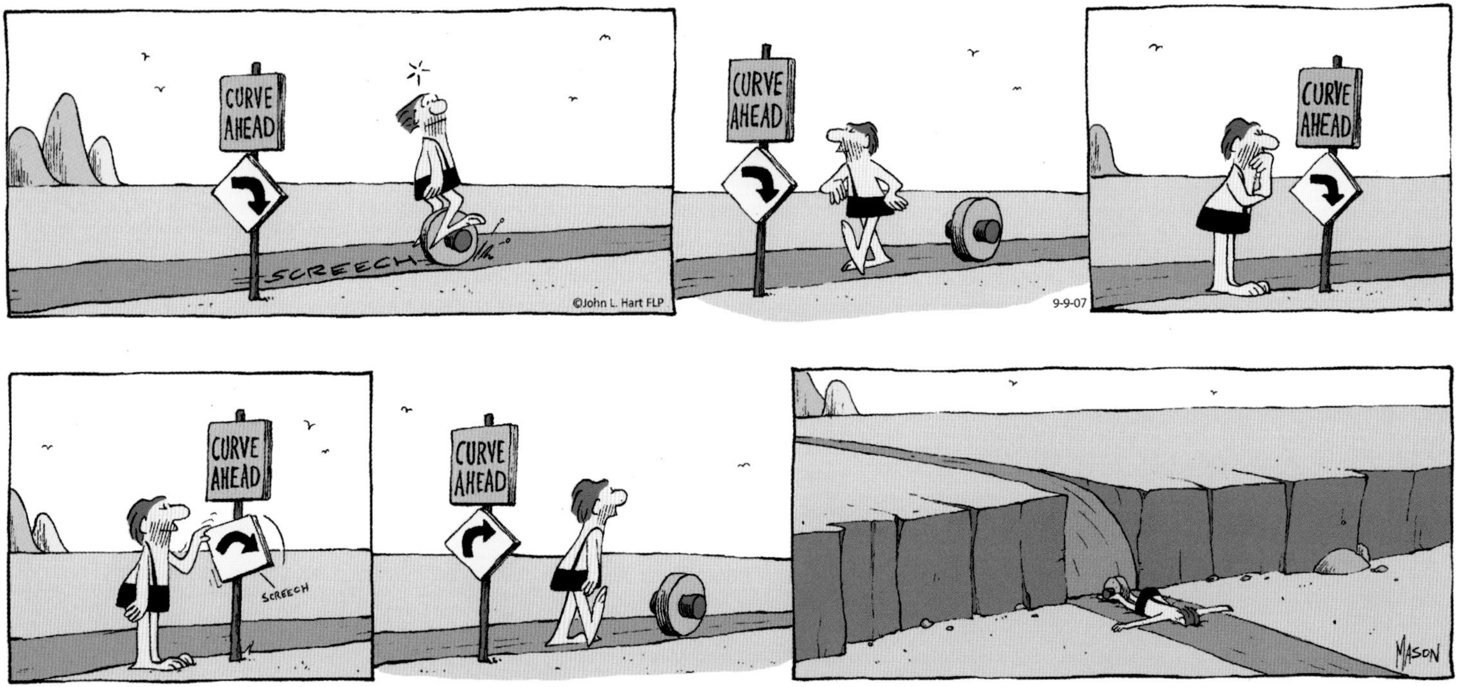
CURVE AHEAD
SCREECH
©John L. Hart FLP
CURVE AHEAD
9-9-07
CURVE AHEAD
CURVE AHEAD
SCREECH
CURVE AHEAD
MASON

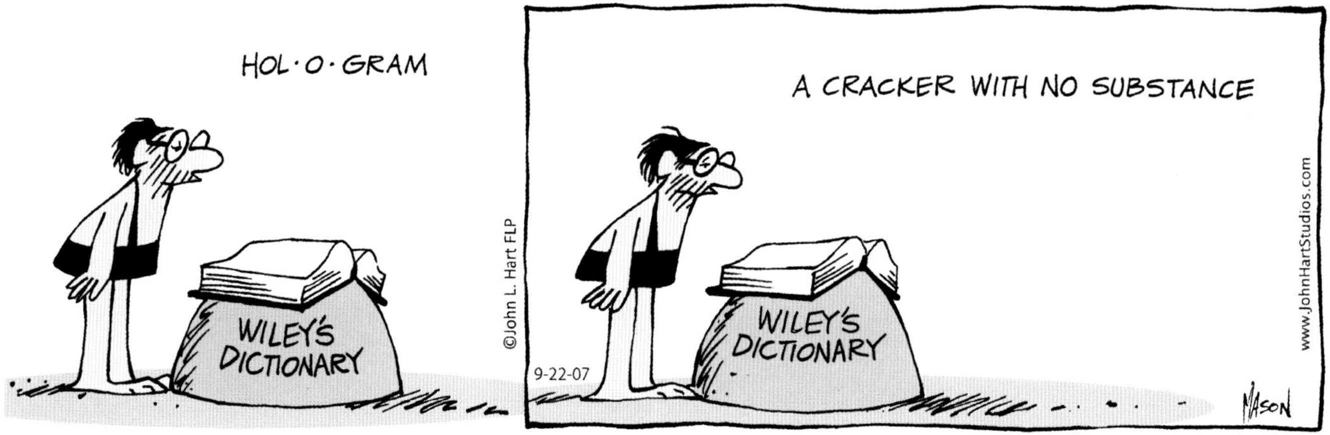
HOL·O·GRAM
WILEY'S DICTIONARY
©John L. Hart FLP
9-22-07
A CRACKER WITH NO SUBSTANCE
WILEY'S DICTIONARY
www.JohnHartStudios.com
MASON

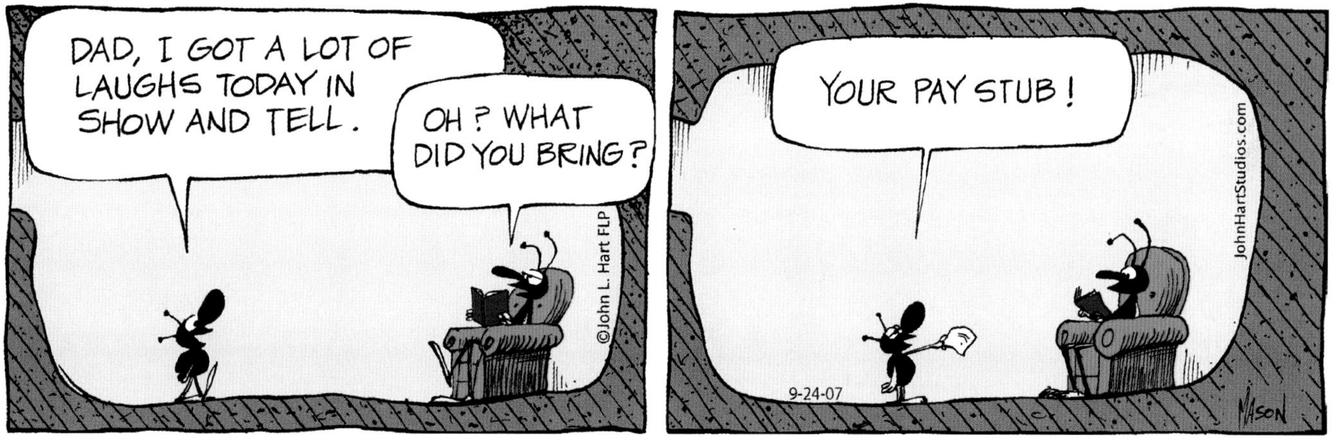
DAD, I GOT A LOT OF LAUGHS TODAY IN SHOW AND TELL.
OH? WHAT DID YOU BRING?
©John L. Hart FLP
YOUR PAY STUB!
JohnHartStudios.com
9-24-07
MASON

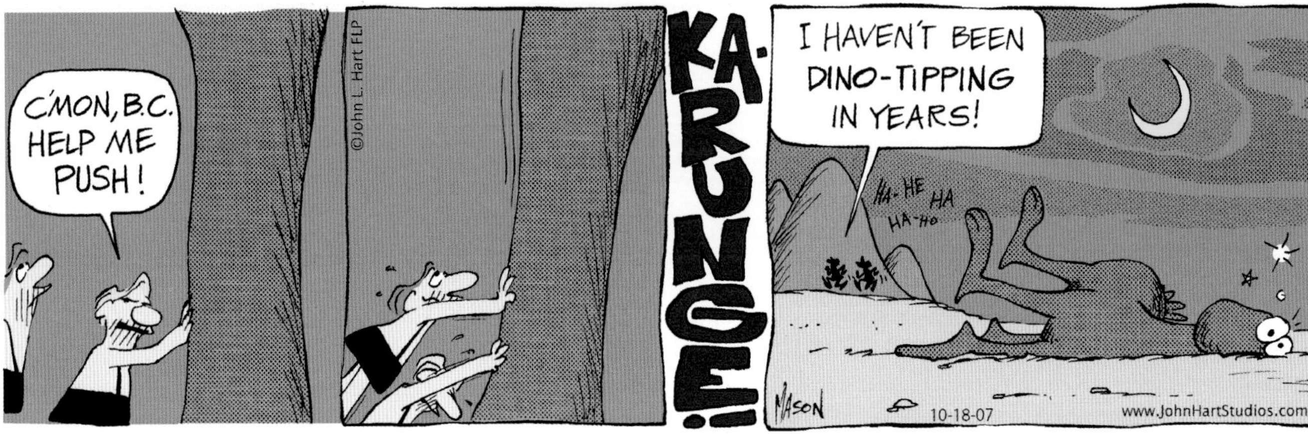
C'MON, B.C. HELP ME PUSH!
©John L. Hart FLP
KA-RUNGE!!
I HAVEN'T BEEN DINO-TIPPING IN YEARS!
HA-HE HA HA-HO
MASON
10-18-07
www.JohnHartStudios.com

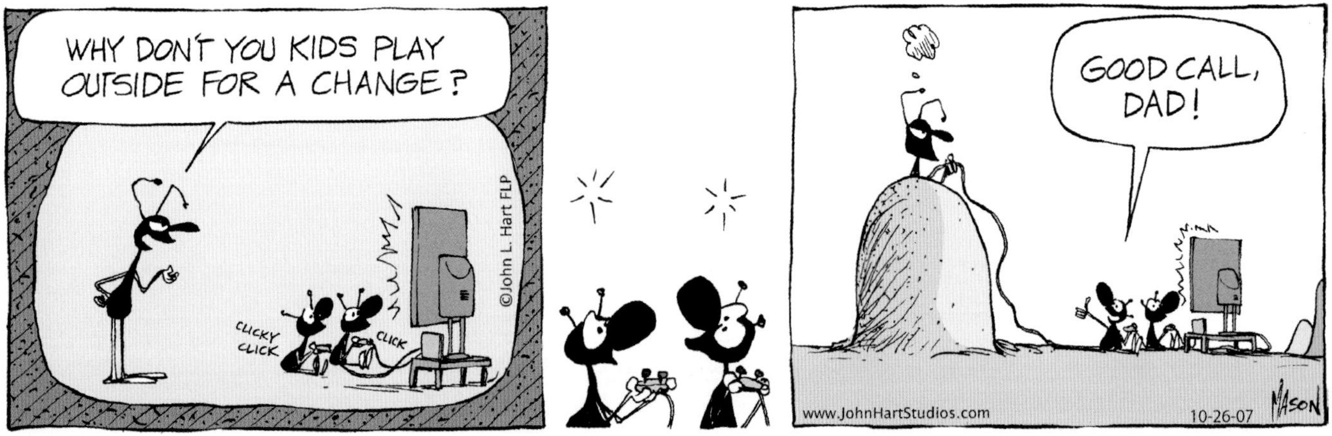
WHY DON'T YOU KIDS PLAY OUTSIDE FOR A CHANGE?
CLICKY CLICK
CLICK
©John L. Hart FLP
GOOD CALL, DAD!
www.JohnHartStudios.com
10-26-07
MASON

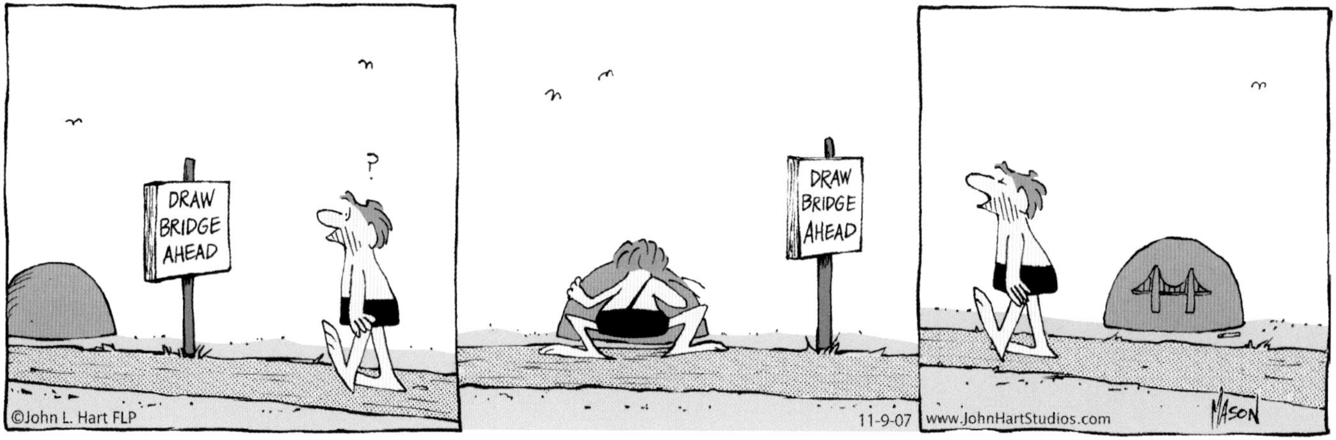
DRAW BRIDGE AHEAD
?
DRAW BRIDGE AHEAD
©John L. Hart FLP
11-9-07
www.JohnHartStudios.com
MASON

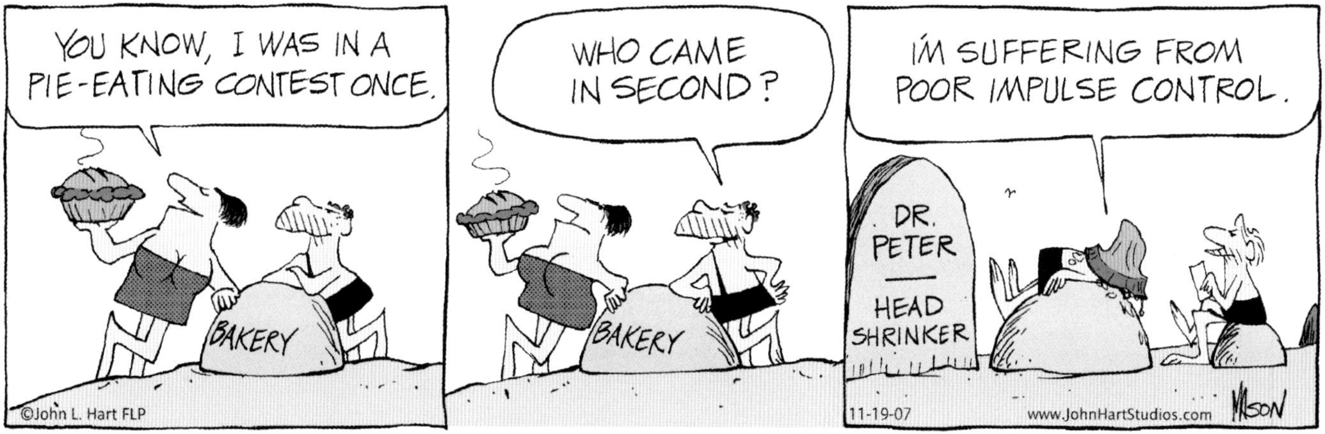
YOU KNOW, I WAS IN A PIE-EATING CONTEST ONCE.
BAKERY
WHO CAME IN SECOND?
BAKERY
I'M SUFFERING FROM POOR IMPULSE CONTROL.
DR. PETER — HEAD SHRINKER
©John L. Hart FLP
11-19-07
www.JohnHartStudios.com
MASON

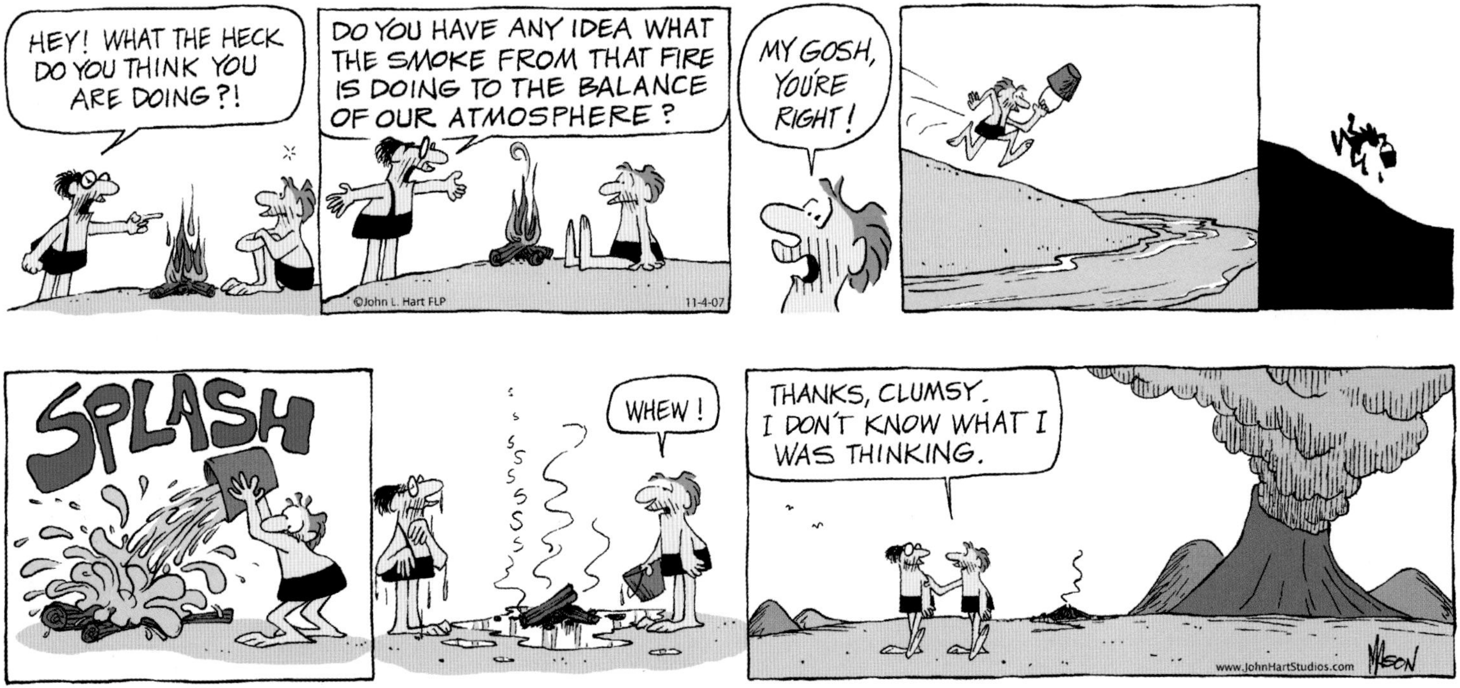
HEY! WHAT THE HECK DO YOU THINK YOU ARE DOING?!
DO YOU HAVE ANY IDEA WHAT THE SMOKE FROM THAT FIRE IS DOING TO THE BALANCE OF OUR ATMOSPHERE?
©John L. Hart FLP
11-4-07
MY GOSH, YOU'RE RIGHT!
SPLASH
WHEW!
THANKS, CLUMSY. I DON'T KNOW WHAT I WAS THINKING.
www.JohnHartStudios.com
MASON

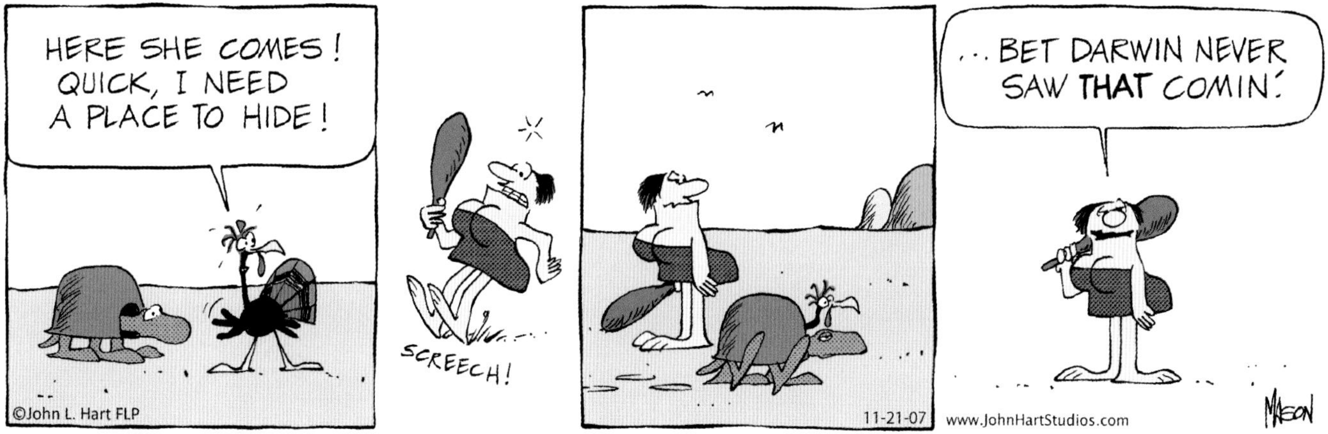
HERE SHE COMES! QUICK, I NEED A PLACE TO HIDE!
SCREECH!
...BET DARWIN NEVER SAW THAT COMIN'.
©John L. Hart FLP
11-21-07
www.JohnHartStudios.com
MASON

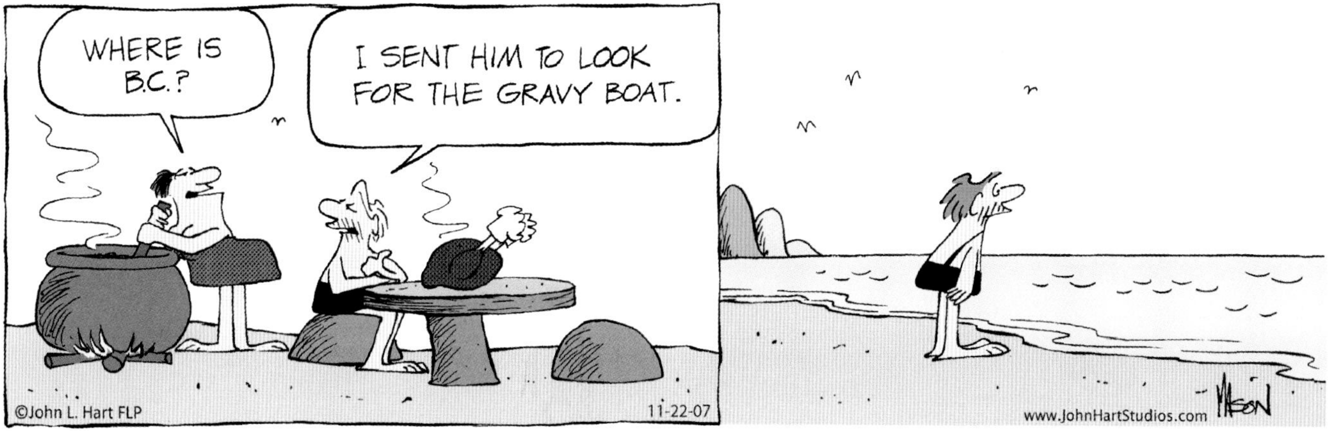
WHERE IS B.C.?
I SENT HIM TO LOOK FOR THE GRAVY BOAT.
©John L. Hart FLP
11-22-07
www.JohnHartStudios.com
MASON

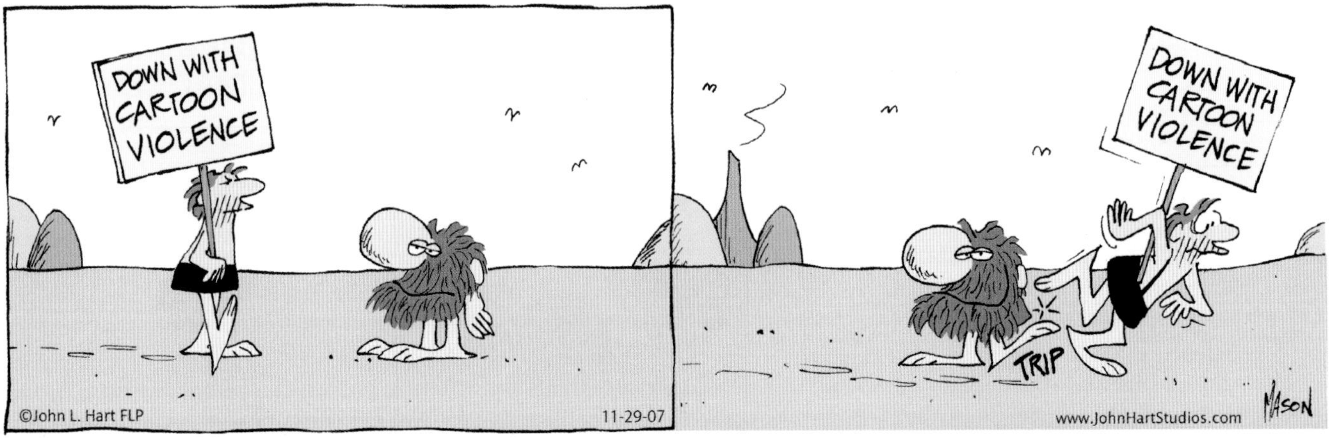
DOWN WITH CARTOON VIOLENCE
©John L. Hart FLP
11-29-07
DOWN WITH CARTOON VIOLENCE
TRIP
www.JohnHartStudios.com
MASON

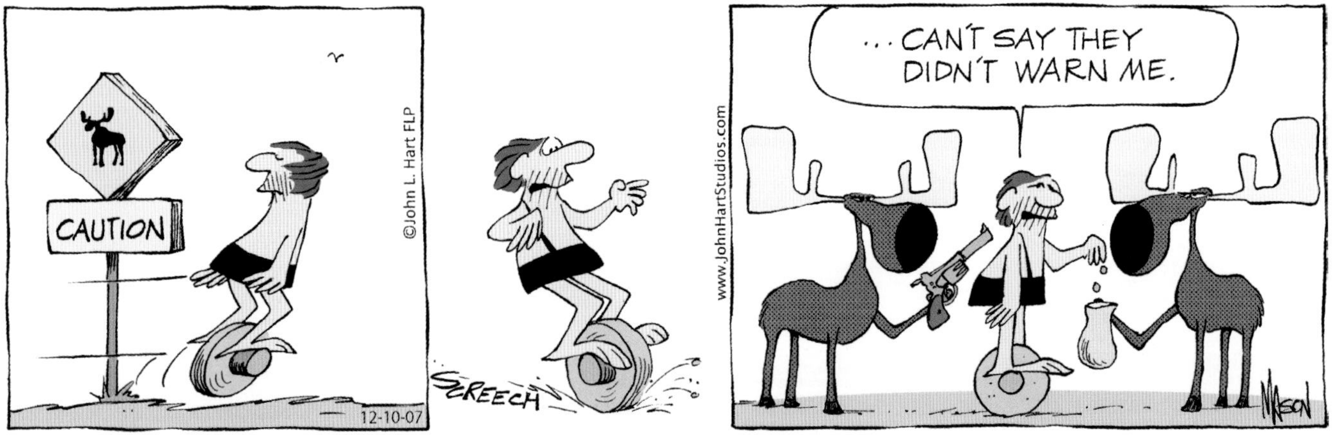
CAUTION
©John L. Hart FLP
12-10-07
SCREECH
www.JohnHartStudios.com
...CAN'T SAY THEY DIDN'T WARN ME.
MASON

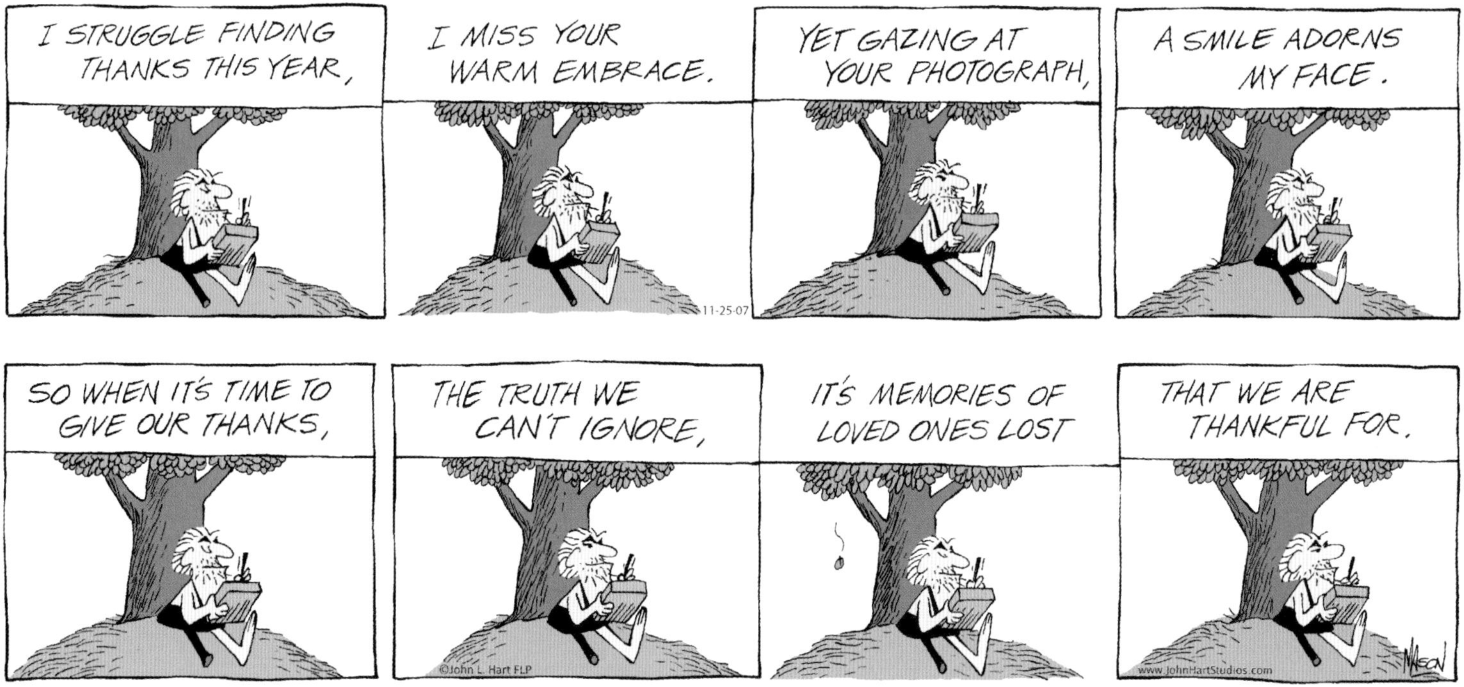
I STRUGGLE FINDING THANKS THIS YEAR,
I MISS YOUR WARM EMBRACE.
YET GAZING AT YOUR PHOTOGRAPH,
A SMILE ADORNS MY FACE.
11-25-07
SO WHEN IT'S TIME TO GIVE OUR THANKS,
THE TRUTH WE CAN'T IGNORE,
IT'S MEMORIES OF LOVED ONES LOST
THAT WE ARE THANKFUL FOR.
©John L. Hart FLP
www.JohnHartStudios.com
MASON

Mason's first Thanksgiving poem honored Johnny's memory. (Look closely at the bark in the panel with the falling leaf)

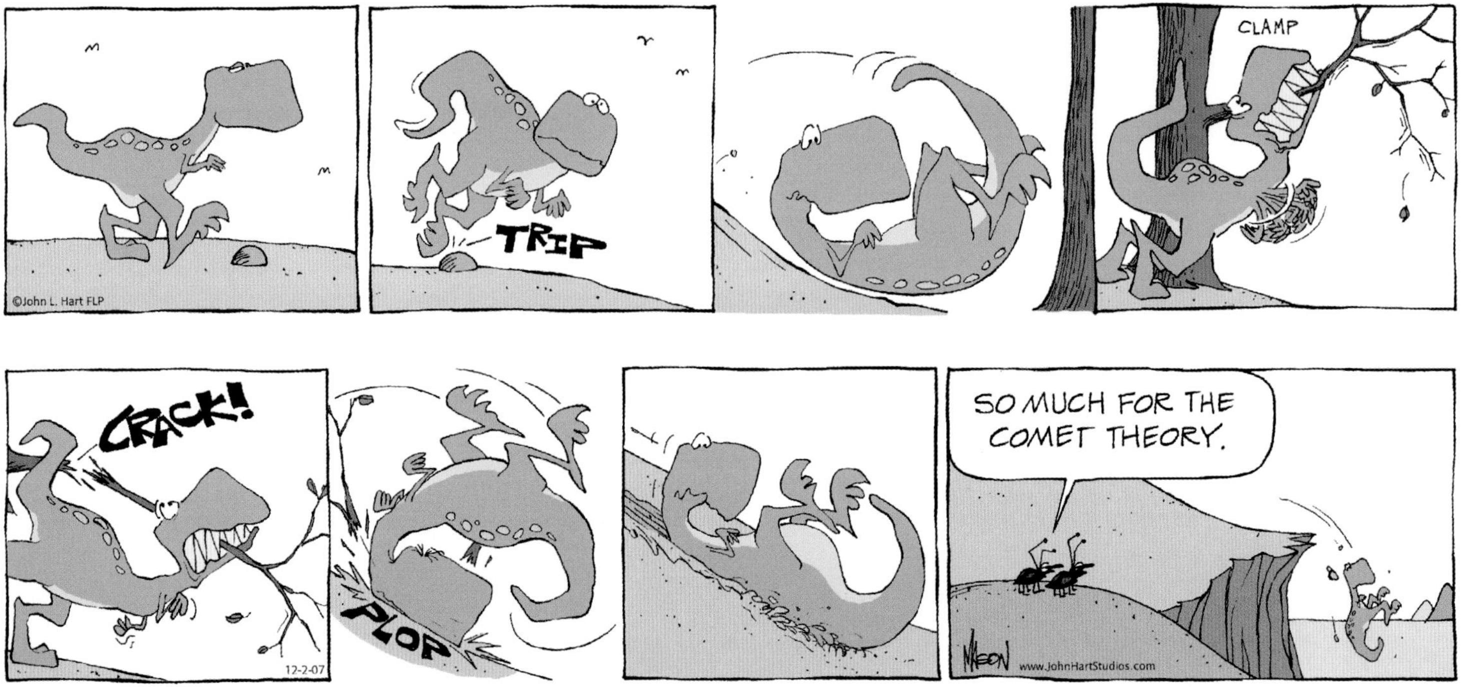
©John L. Hart FLP
TRIP
CLAMP
CRACK!
12-2-07
PLOP
SO MUCH FOR THE COMET THEORY.
www.JohnHartStudios.com

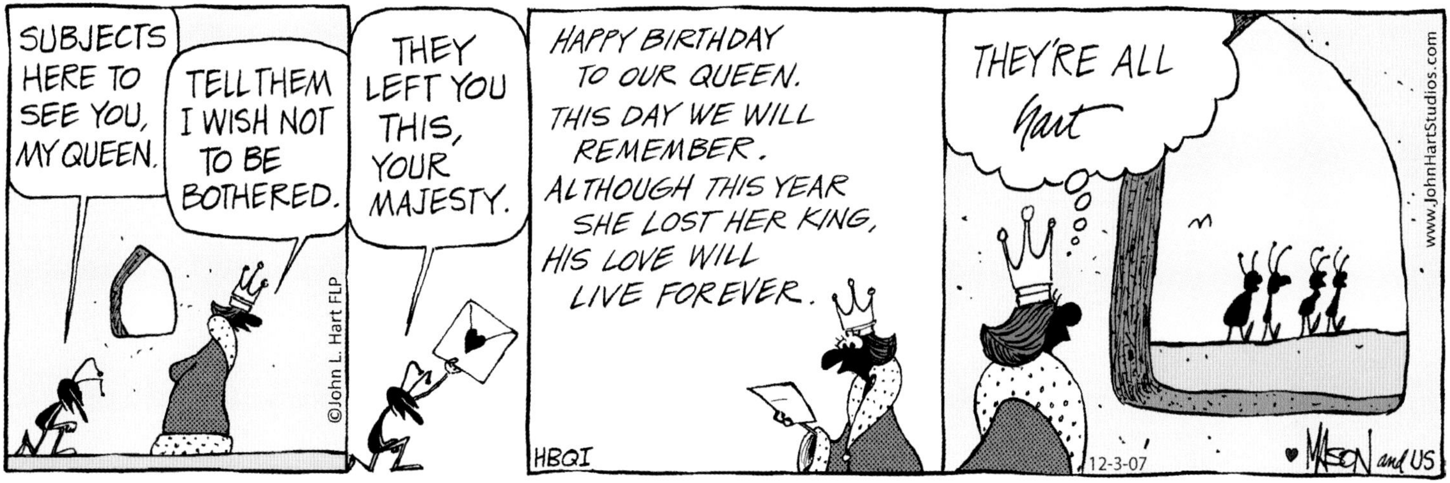
SUBJECTS HERE TO SEE YOU, MY QUEEN.
TELL THEM I WISH NOT TO BE BOTHERED.
THEY LEFT YOU THIS, YOUR MAJESTY.
HAPPY BIRTHDAY TO OUR QUEEN. THIS DAY WE WILL REMEMBER. ALTHOUGH THIS YEAR SHE LOST HER KING, HIS LOVE WILL LIVE FOREVER.
THEY'RE ALL Hart
©John L. Hart FLP
HBQI
12-3-07
MASON and US
www.JohnHartStudios.com

Mason continues to honor his grandmother, Bobby Hart (given name - Ida) on her birthday as Johnny did for 50 years. In the first Queen Ida birthday strip after Johnny passed, the four subjects departing in the final panel are caricatures of (left to right) Mason, Mick, Patti and Perri.

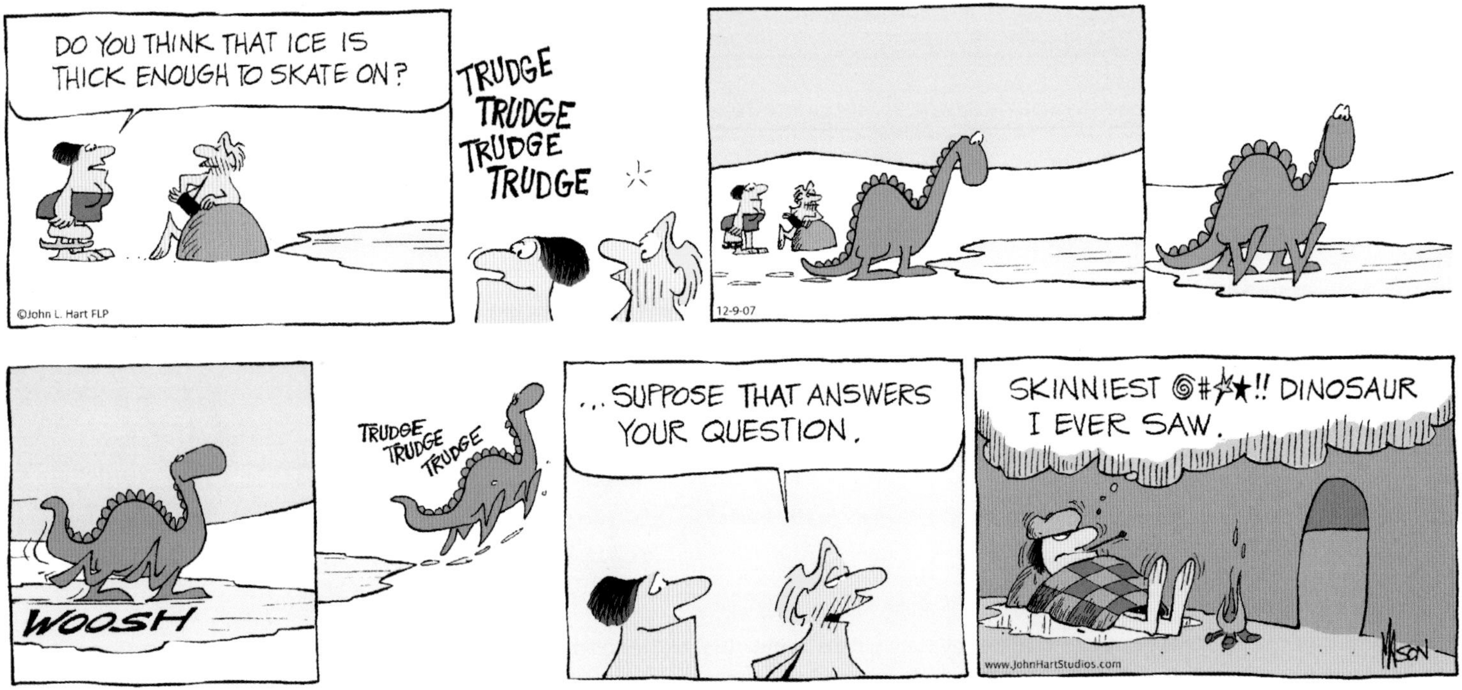
DO YOU THINK THAT ICE IS THICK ENOUGH TO SKATE ON?
©John L. Hart FLP
TRUDGE TRUDGE TRUDGE TRUDGE
12-9-07
WOOSH
TRUDGE TRUDGE TRUDGE
... SUPPOSE THAT ANSWERS YOUR QUESTION.
SKINNIEST @#*★!! DINOSAUR I EVER SAW.
www.JohnHartStudios.com
MASON

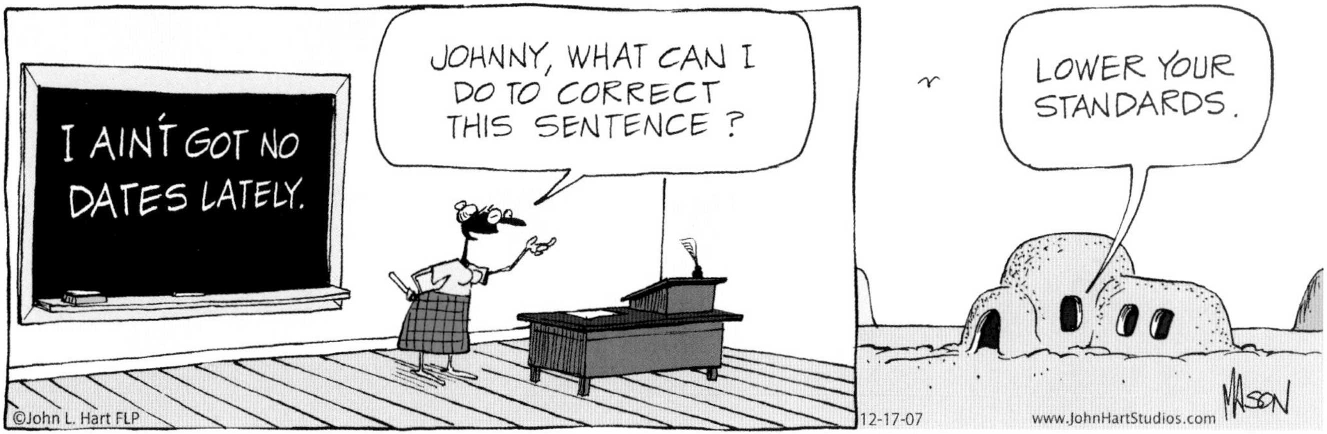
I AIN'T GOT NO DATES LATELY.
JOHNNY, WHAT CAN I DO TO CORRECT THIS SENTENCE ?
LOWER YOUR STANDARDS.
©John L. Hart FLP
12-17-07
www.JohnHartStudios.com
MASON

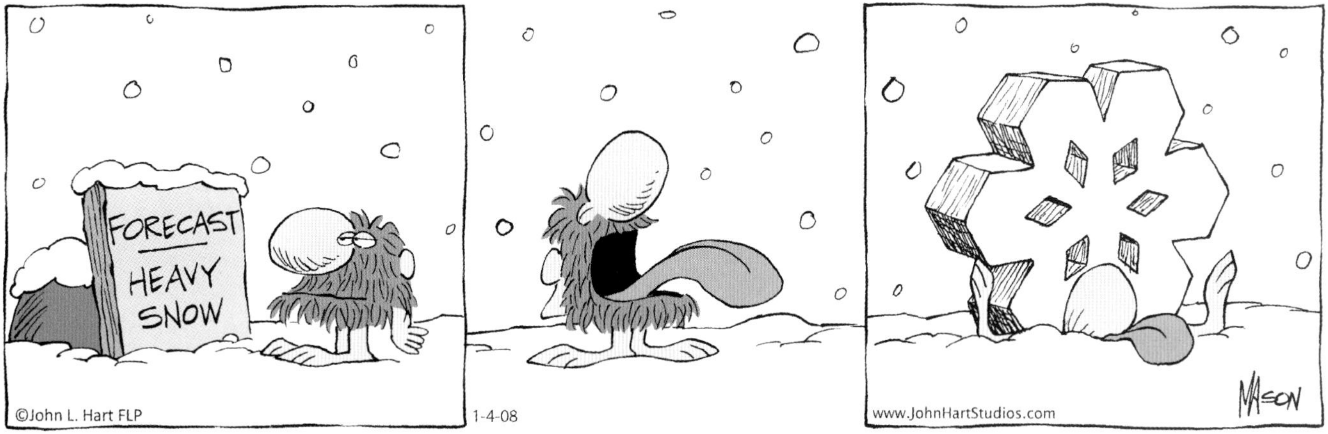
FORECAST
HEAVY SNOW
©John L. Hart FLP
1-4-08
www.JohnHartStudios.com
MASON

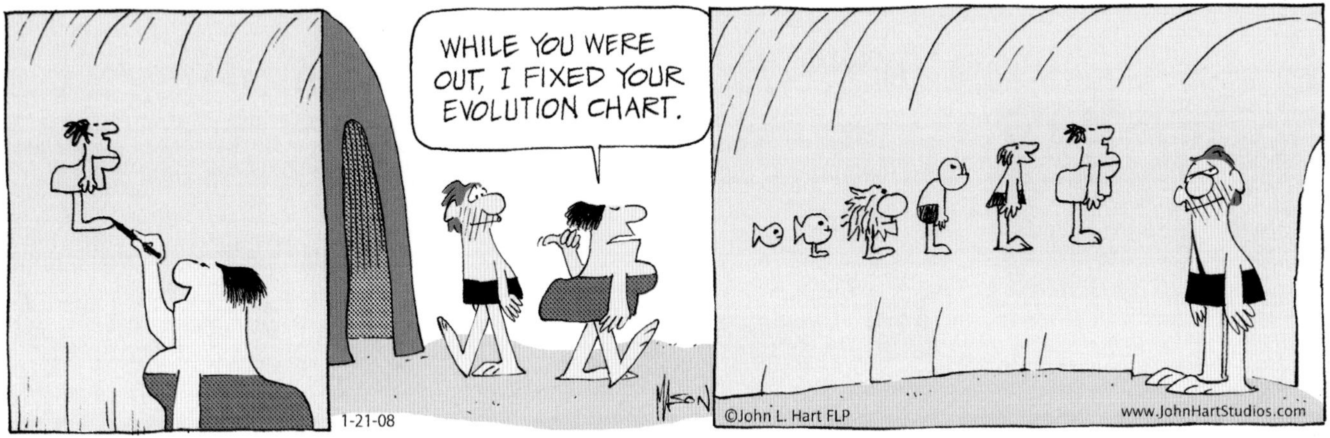
WHILE YOU WERE OUT, I FIXED YOUR EVOLUTION CHART.
1-21-08
MASON
©John L. Hart FLP
www.JohnHartStudios.com

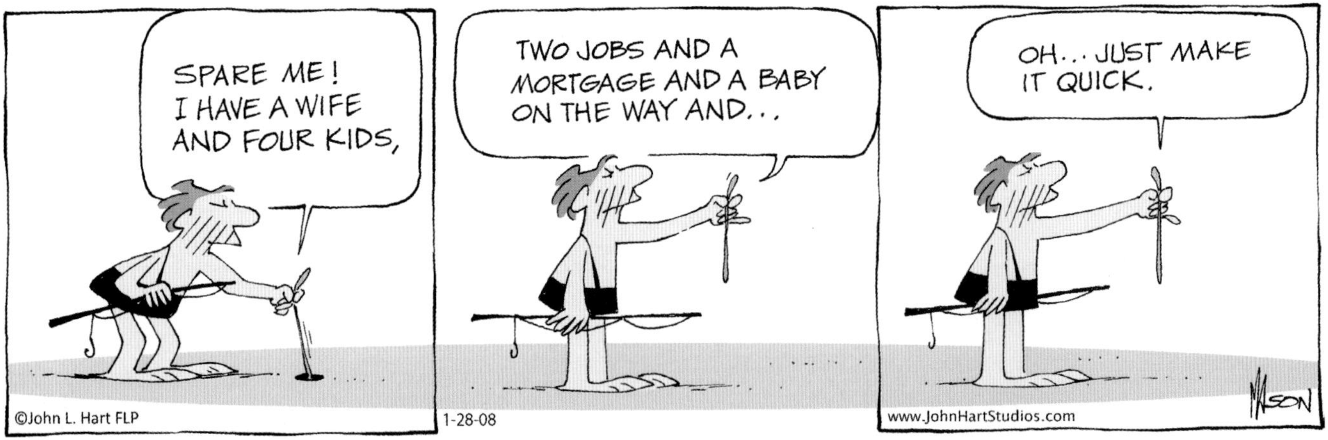
SPARE ME! I HAVE A WIFE AND FOUR KIDS,
TWO JOBS AND A MORTGAGE AND A BABY ON THE WAY AND...
OH... JUST MAKE IT QUICK.
©John L. Hart FLP
1-28-08
www.JohnHartStudios.com
MASON

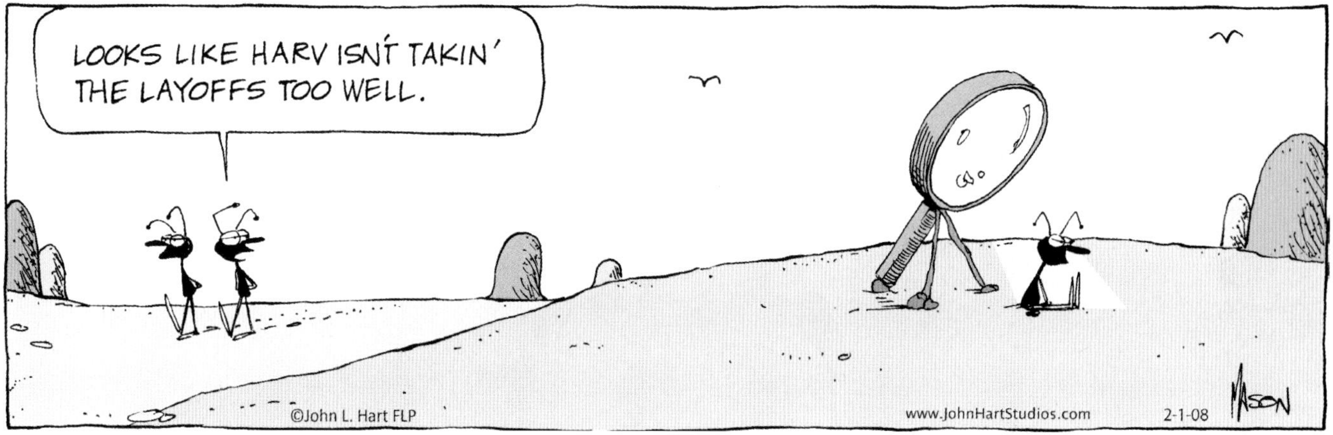

LOOKS LIKE HARV ISN'T TAKIN' THE LAYOFFS TOO WELL.
©John L. Hart FLP
www.JohnHartStudios.com
2-1-08
MASON

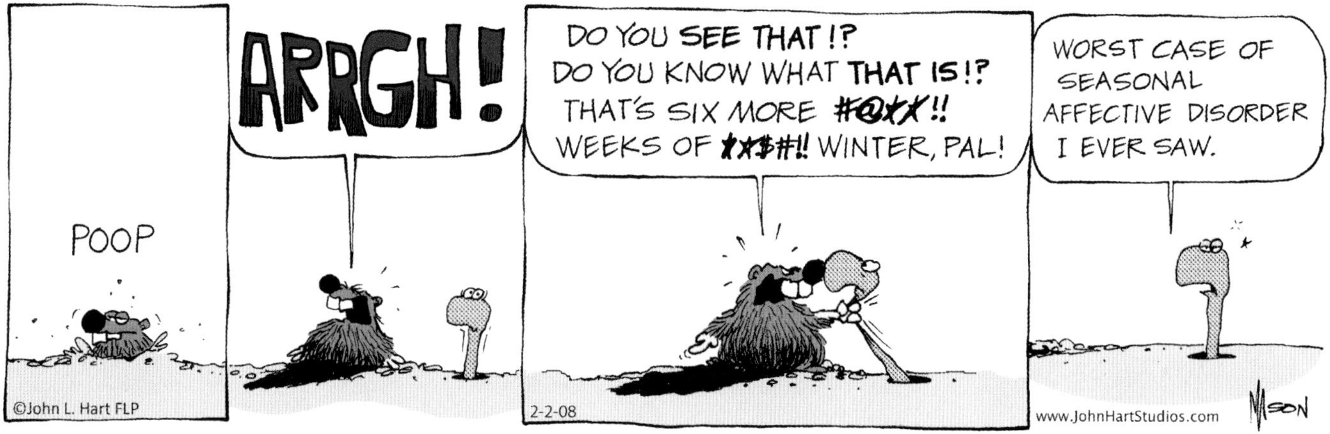

POOP
©John L. Hart FLP
ARRGH!
DO YOU SEE THAT!? DO YOU KNOW WHAT THAT IS!? THAT'S SIX MORE #@✗✗!! WEEKS OF ✗✗$#!! WINTER, PAL!
2-2-08
WORST CASE OF SEASONAL AFFECTIVE DISORDER I EVER SAW.
www.JohnHartStudios.com
MASON

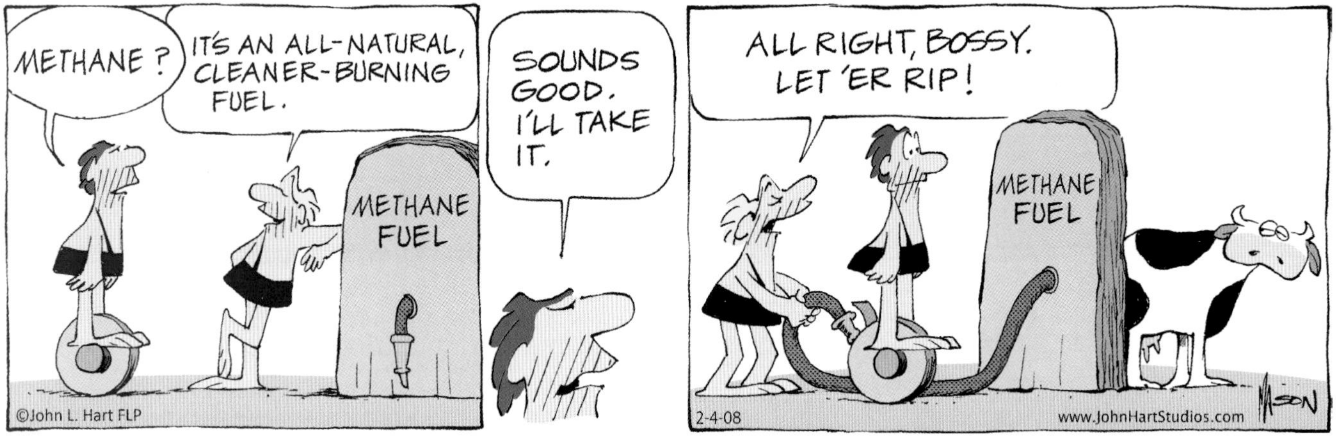
METHANE ?
IT'S AN ALL-NATURAL, CLEANER-BURNING FUEL.
METHANE FUEL
SOUNDS GOOD. I'LL TAKE IT.
ALL RIGHT, BOSSY. LET 'ER RIP!
METHANE FUEL
©John L. Hart FLP
2-4-08
www.JohnHartStudios.com
MASON

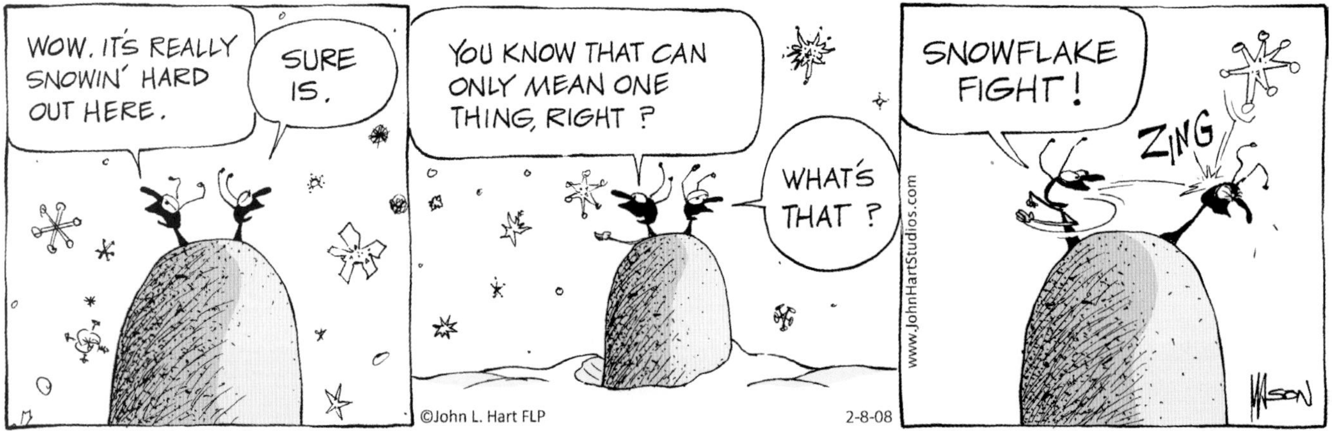
WOW. IT'S REALLY SNOWIN' HARD OUT HERE.
SURE IS.
YOU KNOW THAT CAN ONLY MEAN ONE THING, RIGHT ?
WHAT'S THAT ?
SNOWFLAKE FIGHT!
ZING
©John L. Hart FLP
2-8-08
www.JohnHartStudios.com
MASON

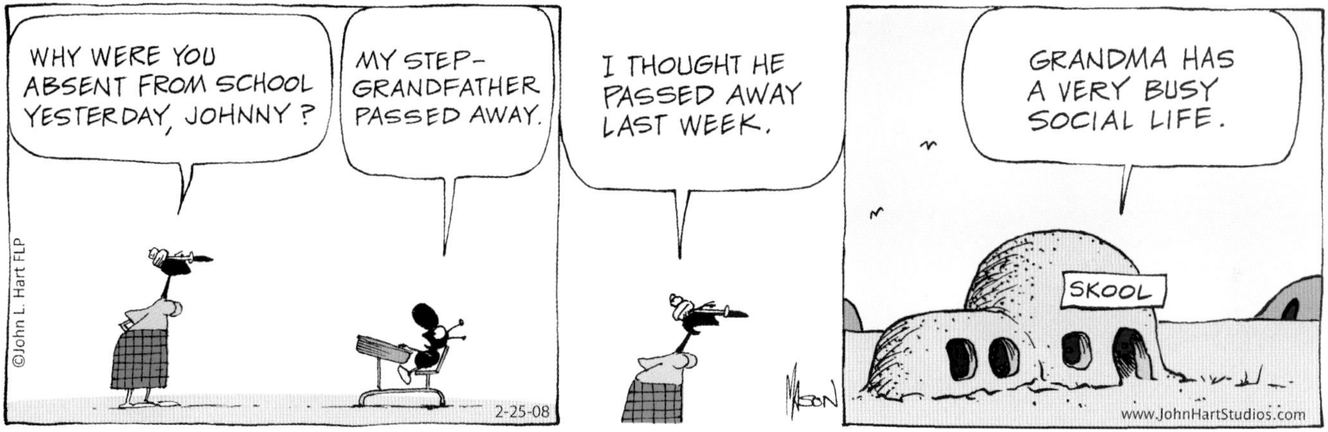
WHY WERE YOU ABSENT FROM SCHOOL YESTERDAY, JOHNNY ?
MY STEP-GRANDFATHER PASSED AWAY.
I THOUGHT HE PASSED AWAY LAST WEEK.
GRANDMA HAS A VERY BUSY SOCIAL LIFE.
SKOOL
©John L. Hart FLP
2-25-08
MASON
www.JohnHartStudios.com

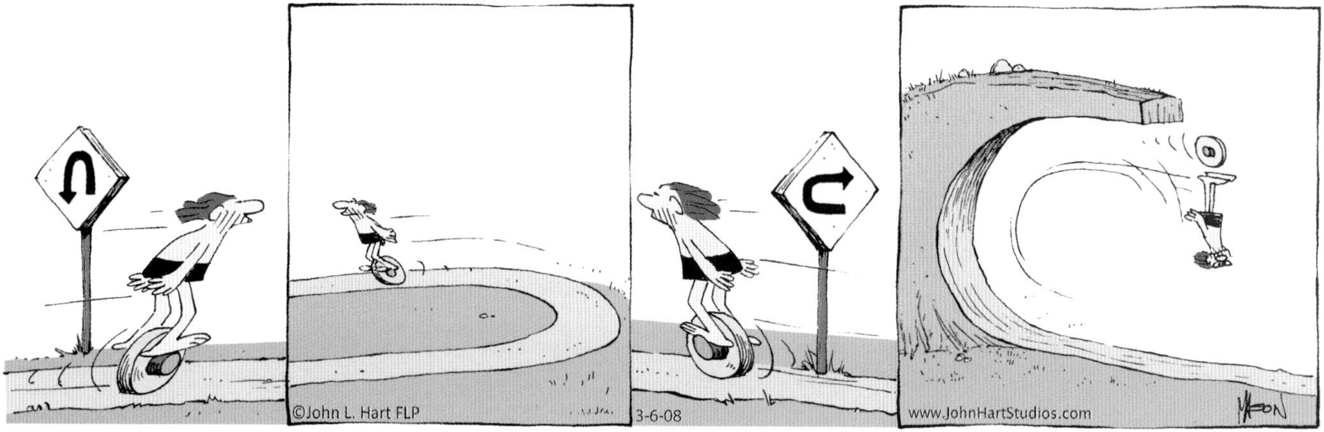
©John L. Hart FLP
3-6-08
www.JohnHartStudios.com
MASON

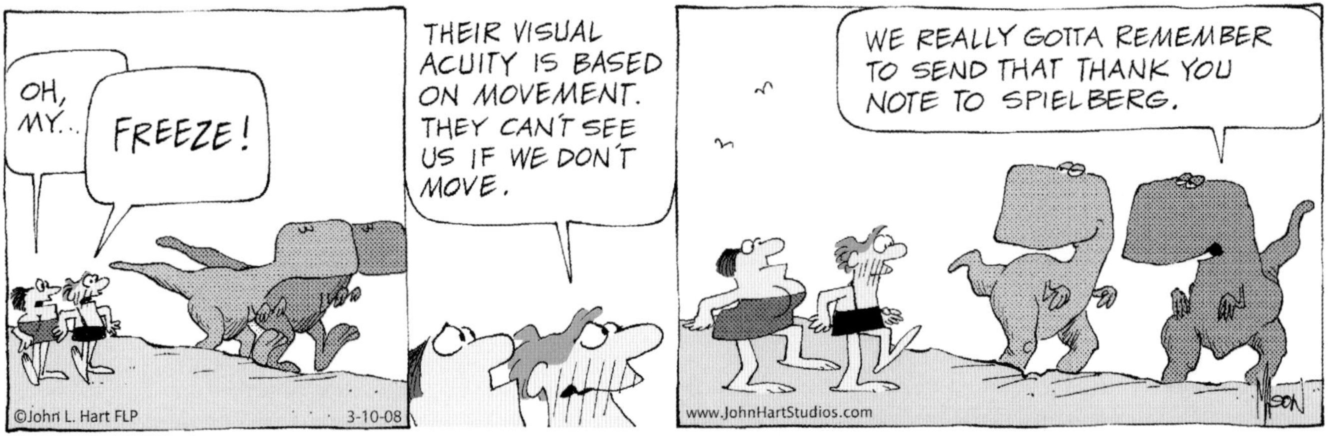
OH, MY...
FREEZE!
THEIR VISUAL ACUITY IS BASED ON MOVEMENT. THEY CAN'T SEE US IF WE DON'T MOVE.
WE REALLY GOTTA REMEMBER TO SEND THAT THANK YOU NOTE TO SPIELBERG.
©John L. Hart FLP
3-10-08
www.JohnHartStudios.com
MASON

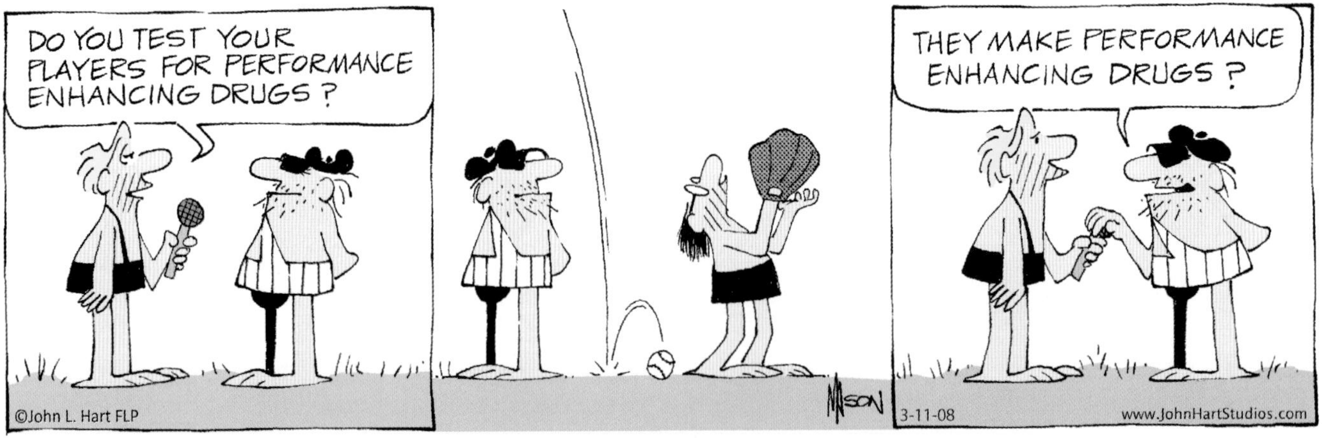
DO YOU TEST YOUR PLAYERS FOR PERFORMANCE ENHANCING DRUGS?
THEY MAKE PERFORMANCE ENHANCING DRUGS?
©John L. Hart FLP
MASON
3-11-08
www.JohnHartStudios.com

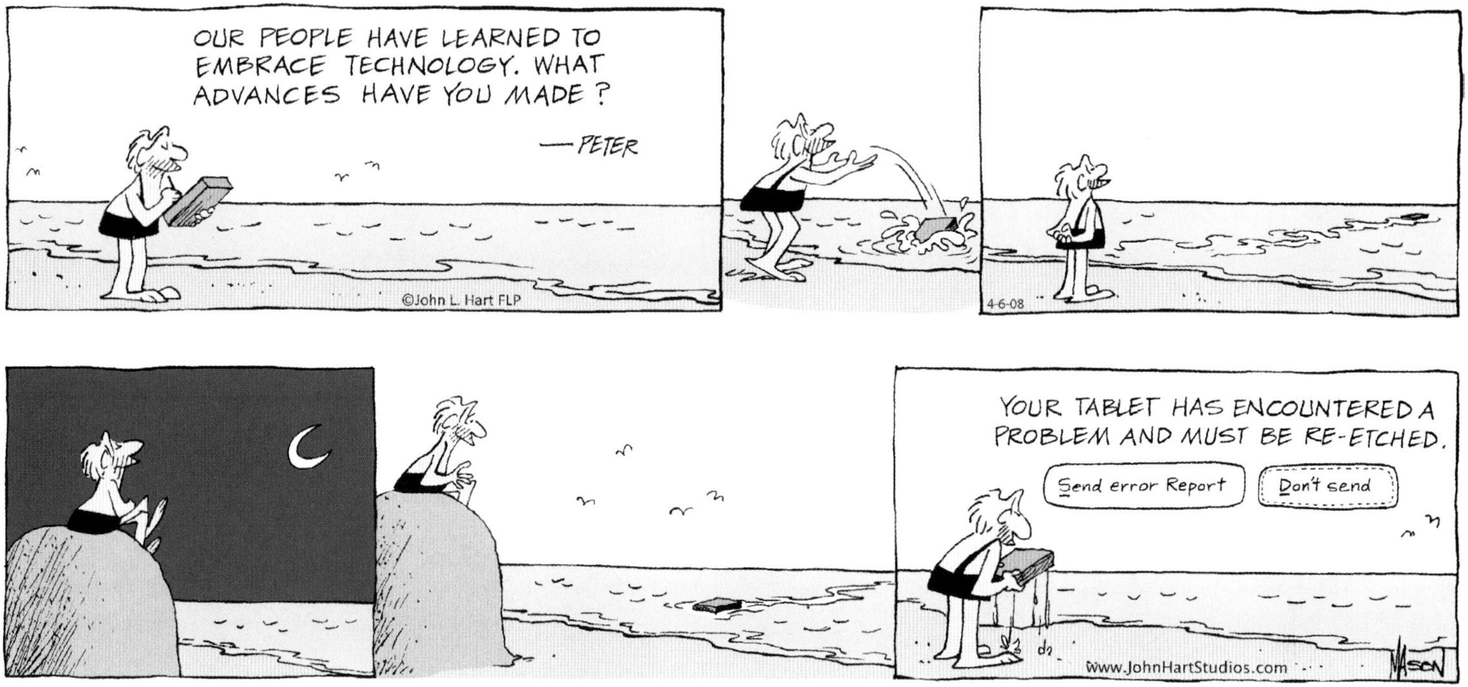
OUR PEOPLE HAVE LEARNED TO EMBRACE TECHNOLOGY. WHAT ADVANCES HAVE YOU MADE?
— PETER
©John L. Hart FLP
4-6-08
YOUR TABLET HAS ENCOUNTERED A PROBLEM AND MUST BE RE-ETCHED.
Send error Report
Don't send
www.JohnHartStudios.com
MASON

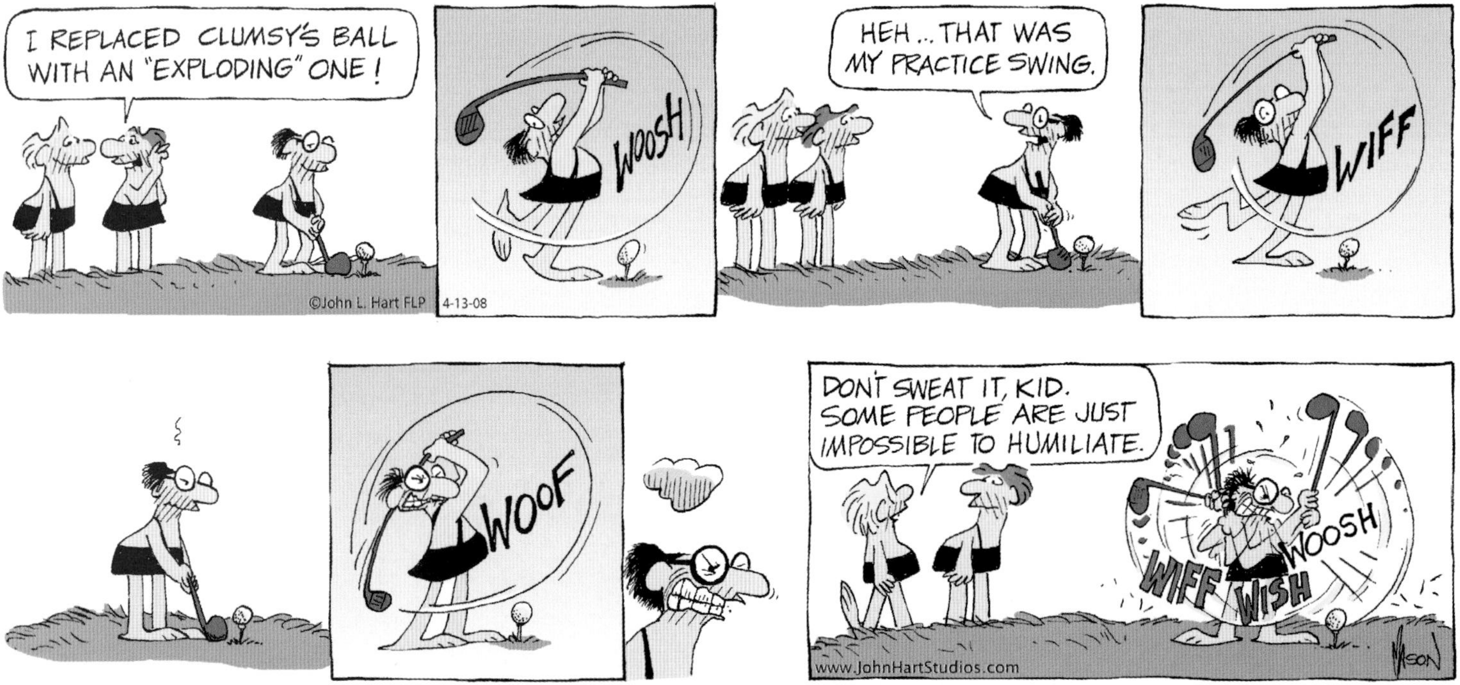
I REPLACED CLUMSY'S BALL WITH AN "EXPLODING" ONE!
©John L. Hart FLP
4-13-08
WOOSH
HEH... THAT WAS MY PRACTICE SWING.
WIFF
WOOF
DON'T SWEAT IT, KID. SOME PEOPLE ARE JUST IMPOSSIBLE TO HUMILIATE.
WIFF
WISH
WOOSH
MASON
www.JohnHartStudios.com

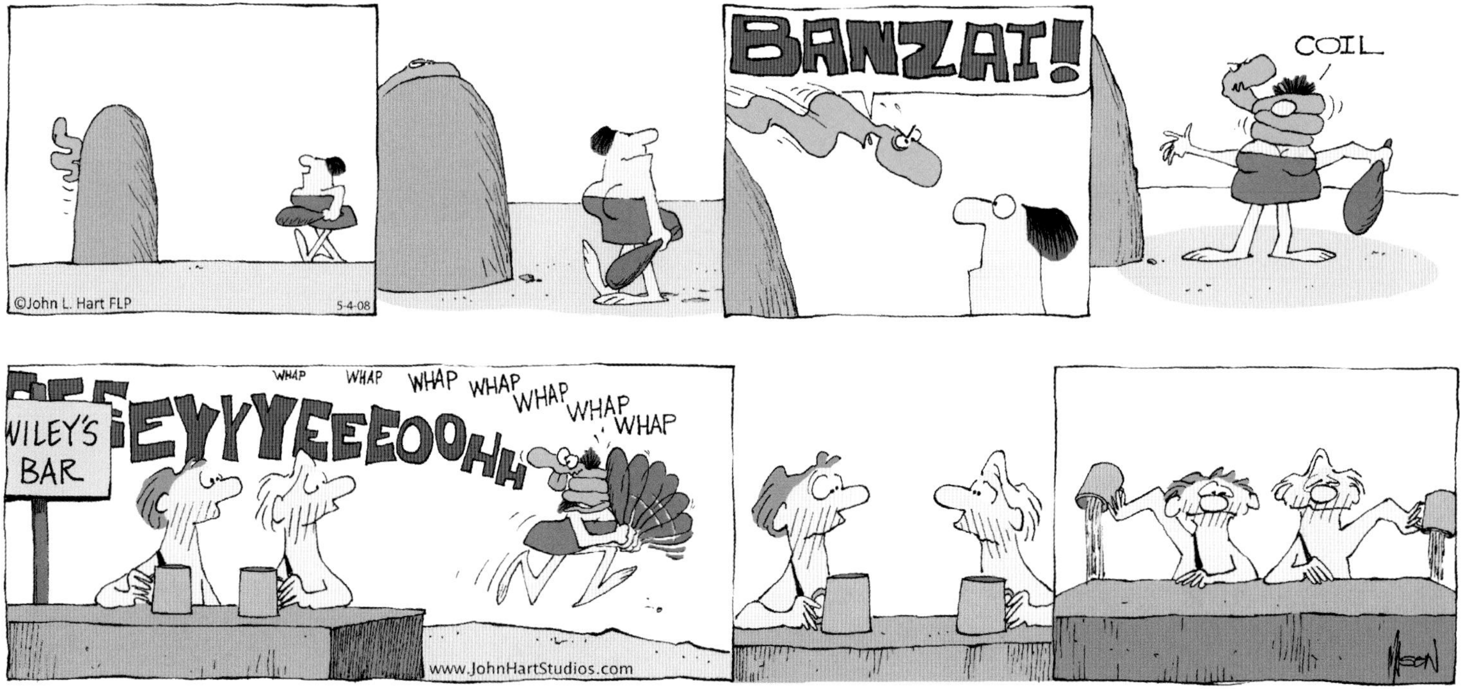
©John L. Hart FLP
5-4-08
BANZAI!
COIL
WILEY'S BAR
EYYYEEEEOOHH
WHAP WHAP WHAP WHAP WHAP WHAP WHAP
www.JohnHartStudios.com

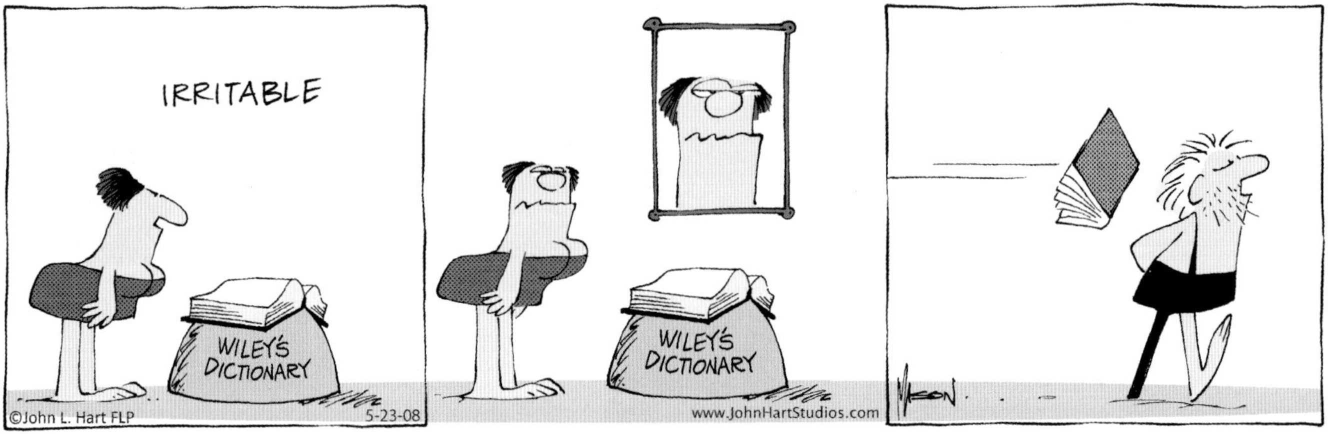
IRRITABLE
WILEY'S DICTIONARY
©John L. Hart FLP
5-23-08
WILEY'S DICTIONARY
www.JohnHartStudios.com

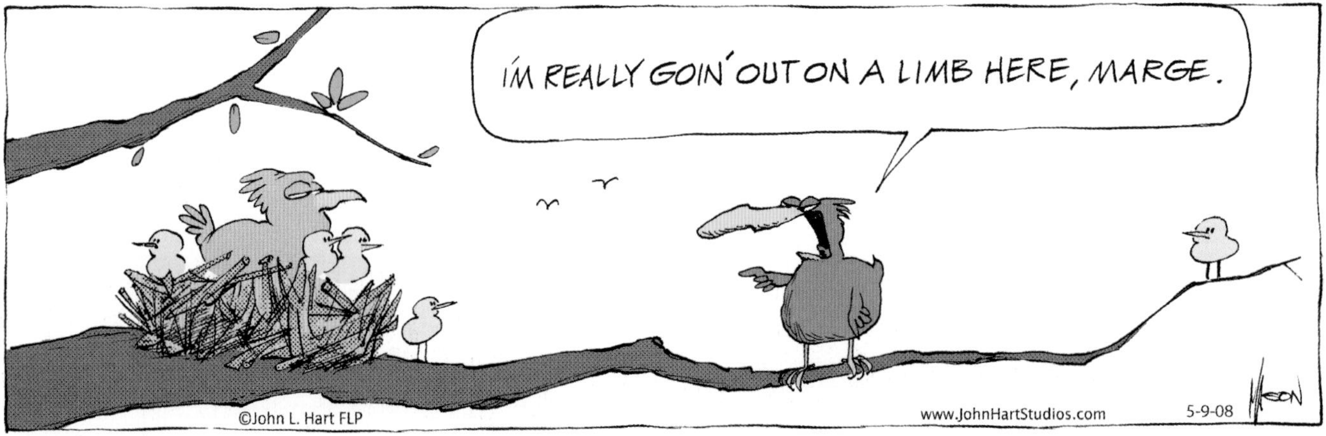
I'M REALLY GOIN' OUT ON A LIMB HERE, MARGE.
©John L. Hart FLP
www.JohnHartStudios.com
5-9-08

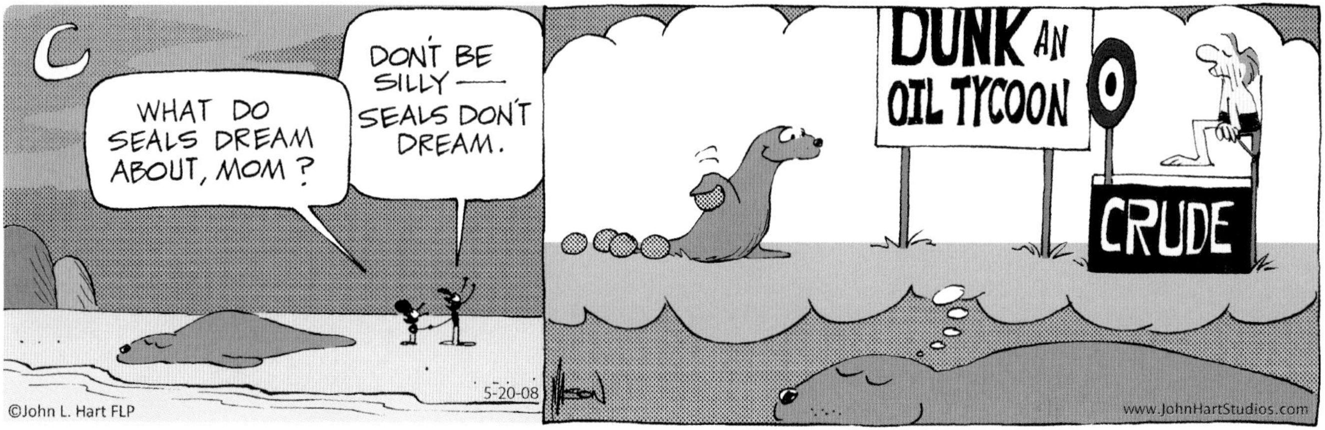
WHAT DO SEALS DREAM ABOUT, MOM?
DON'T BE SILLY — SEALS DON'T DREAM.
DUNK AN OIL TYCOON
CRUDE
5-20-08
©John L. Hart FLP
www.JohnHartStudios.com

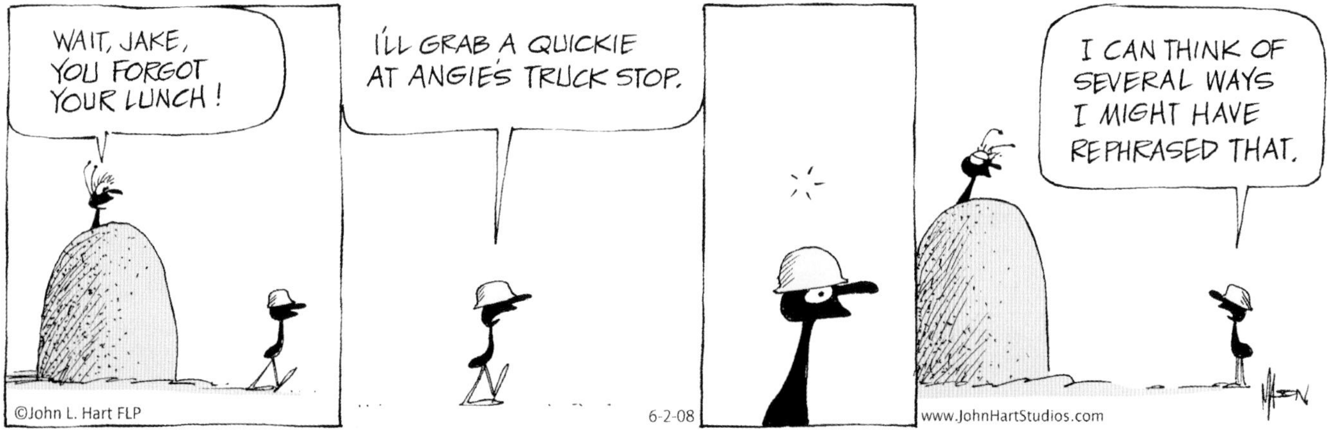
WAIT, JAKE, YOU FORGOT YOUR LUNCH!
I'LL GRAB A QUICKIE AT ANGIE'S TRUCK STOP.
I CAN THINK OF SEVERAL WAYS I MIGHT HAVE REPHRASED THAT.
©John L. Hart FLP
6-2-08
www.JohnHartStudios.com

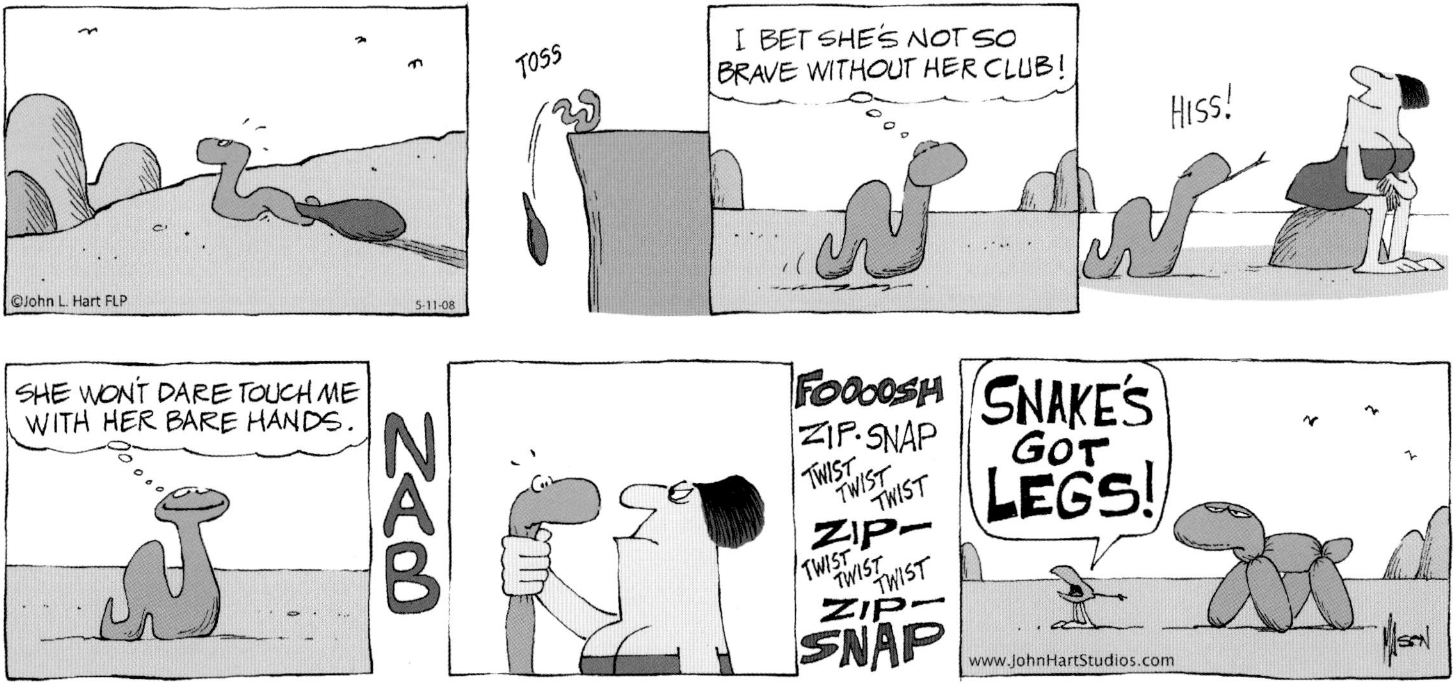
©John L. Hart FLP
5-11-08
TOSS
I BET SHE'S NOT SO BRAVE WITHOUT HER CLUB!
HISS!
SHE WON'T DARE TOUCH ME WITH HER BARE HANDS.
NAB
FOOOOSH
ZIP·SNAP
TWIST TWIST TWIST
ZIP—
TWIST TWIST TWIST
ZIP—
SNAP
SNAKE'S GOT LEGS!
www.JohnHartStudios.com

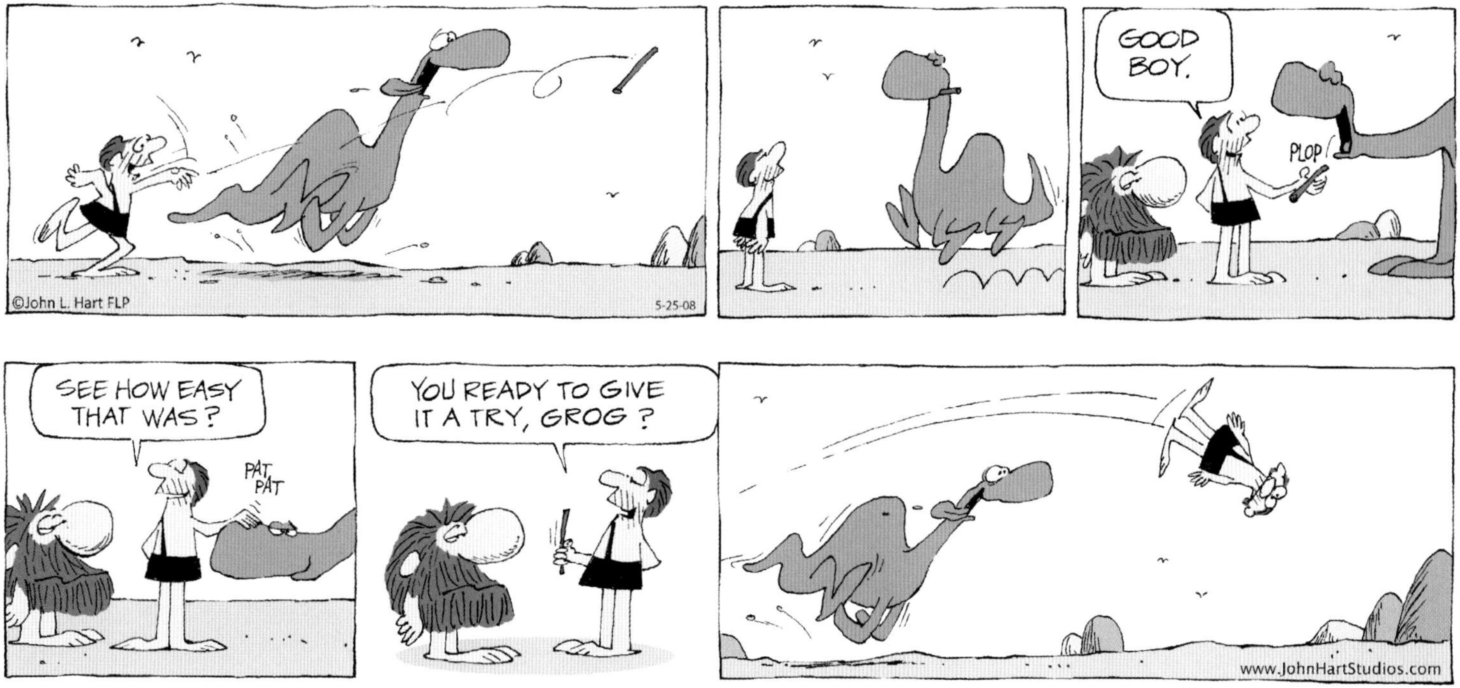
©John L. Hart FLP
5-25-08
GOOD BOY.
PLOP!
SEE HOW EASY THAT WAS?
PAT PAT
YOU READY TO GIVE IT A TRY, GROG?
www.JohnHartStudios.com

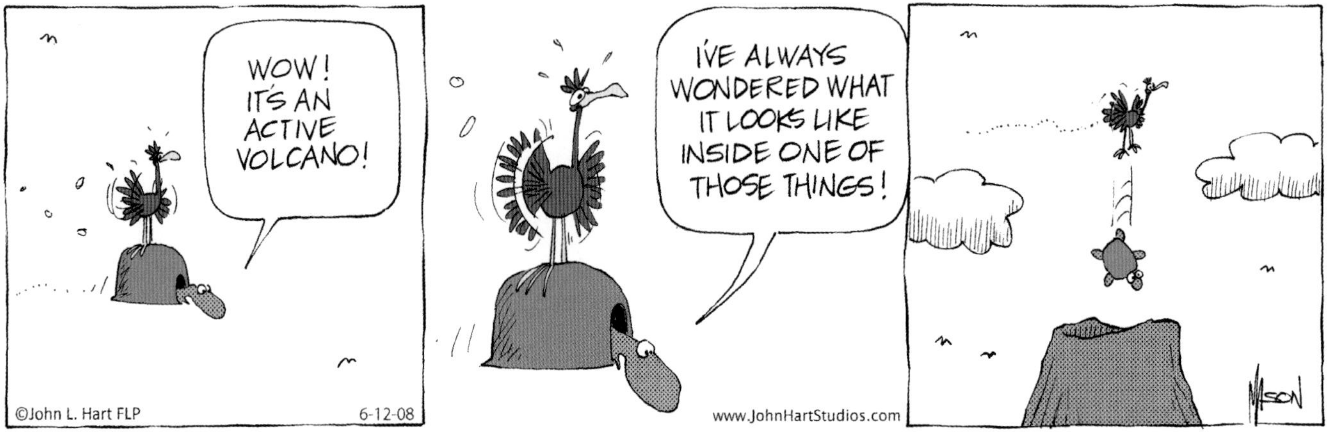
WOW! IT'S AN ACTIVE VOLCANO!
I'VE ALWAYS WONDERED WHAT IT LOOKS LIKE INSIDE ONE OF THOSE THINGS!
©John L. Hart FLP
6-12-08
www.JohnHartStudios.com

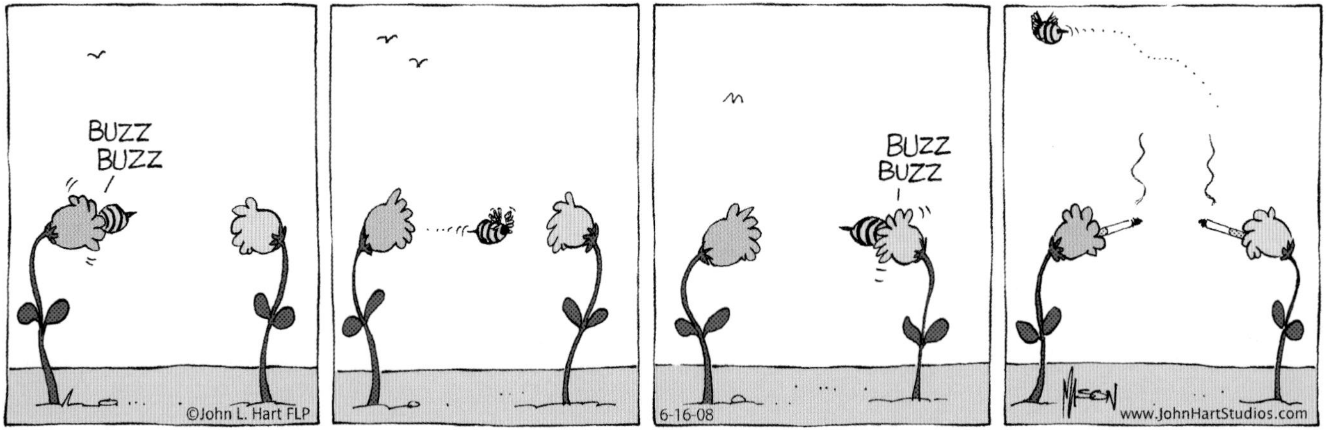
BUZZ BUZZ
©John L. Hart FLP
BUZZ BUZZ
6-16-08
www.JohnHartStudios.com

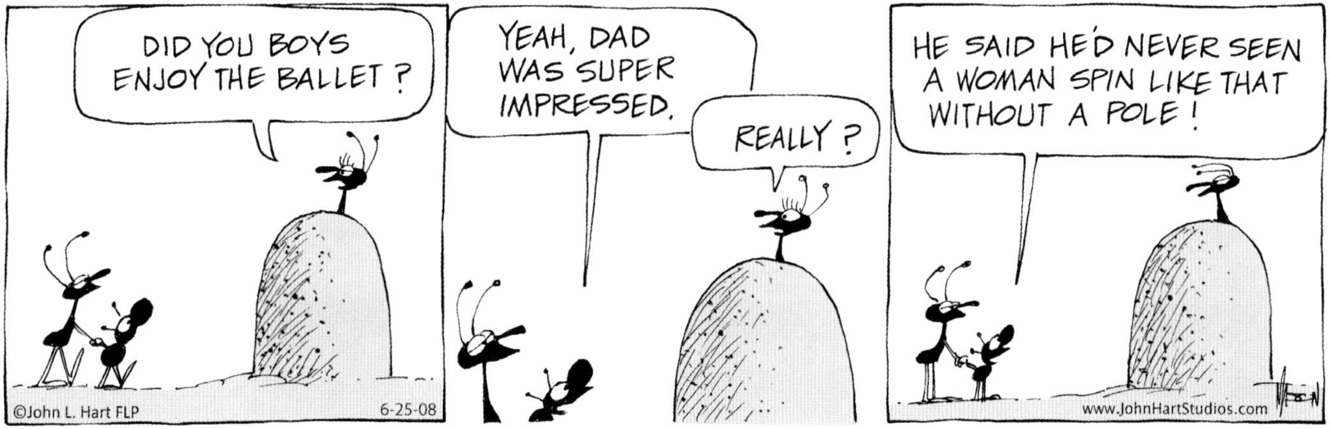
DID YOU BOYS ENJOY THE BALLET ?
YEAH, DAD WAS SUPER IMPRESSED.
REALLY ?
HE SAID HE'D NEVER SEEN A WOMAN SPIN LIKE THAT WITHOUT A POLE !
©John L. Hart FLP
6-25-08
www.JohnHartStudios.com

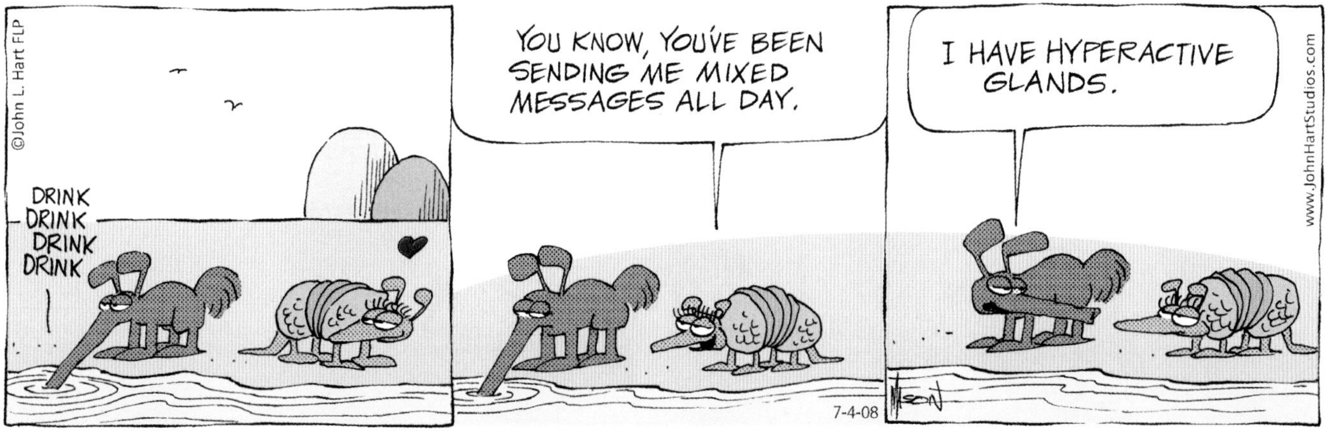
©John L. Hart FLP
DRINK DRINK DRINK DRINK
YOU KNOW, YOU'VE BEEN SENDING ME MIXED MESSAGES ALL DAY.
I HAVE HYPERACTIVE GLANDS.
7-4-08
www.JohnHartStudios.com

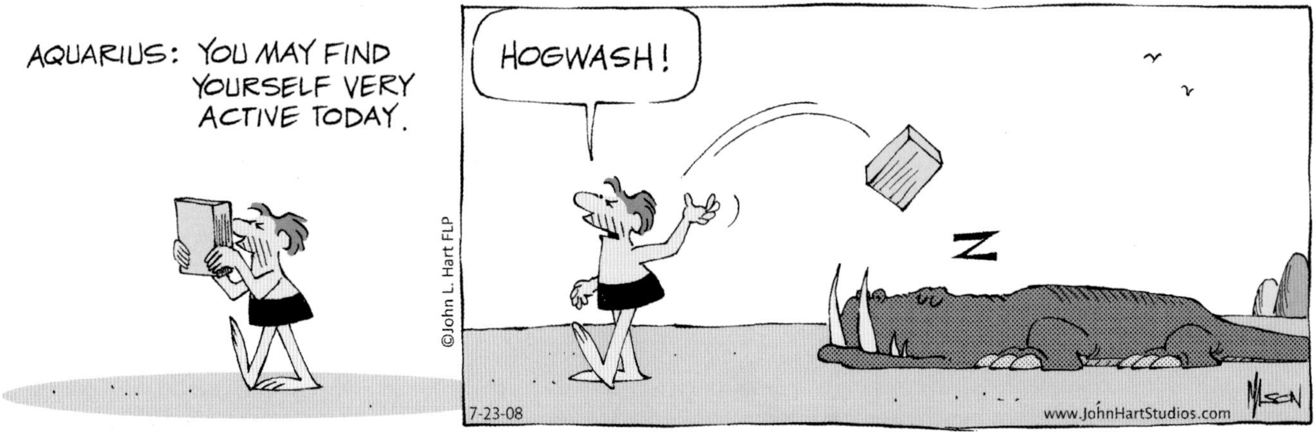
AQUARIUS: YOU MAY FIND YOURSELF VERY ACTIVE TODAY.
HOGWASH!
Z
©John L. Hart FLP
7-23-08
www.JohnHartStudios.com

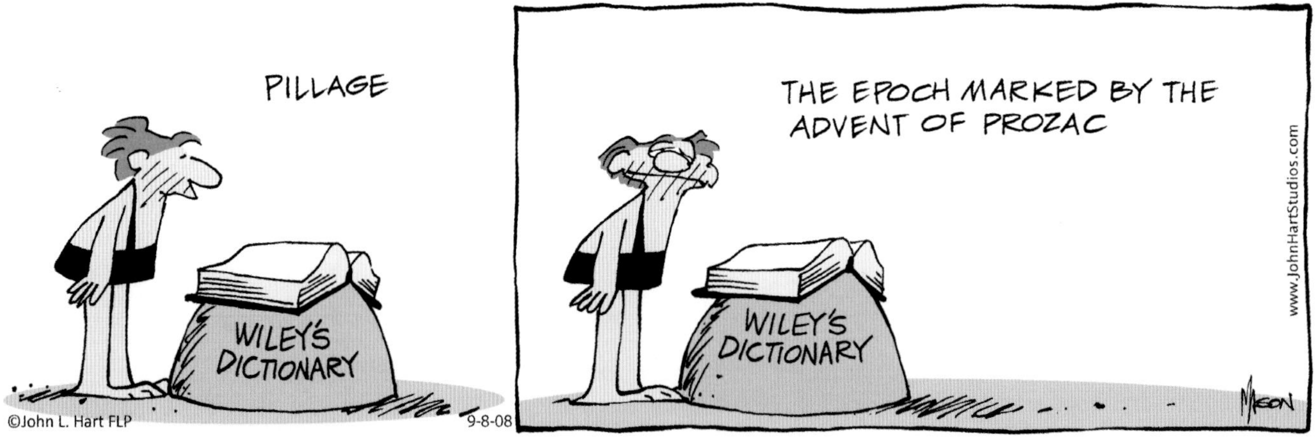
PILLAGE
WILEY'S DICTIONARY
©John L. Hart FLP
THE EPOCH MARKED BY THE ADVENT OF PROZAC
WILEY'S DICTIONARY
9-8-08
www.JohnHartStudios.com

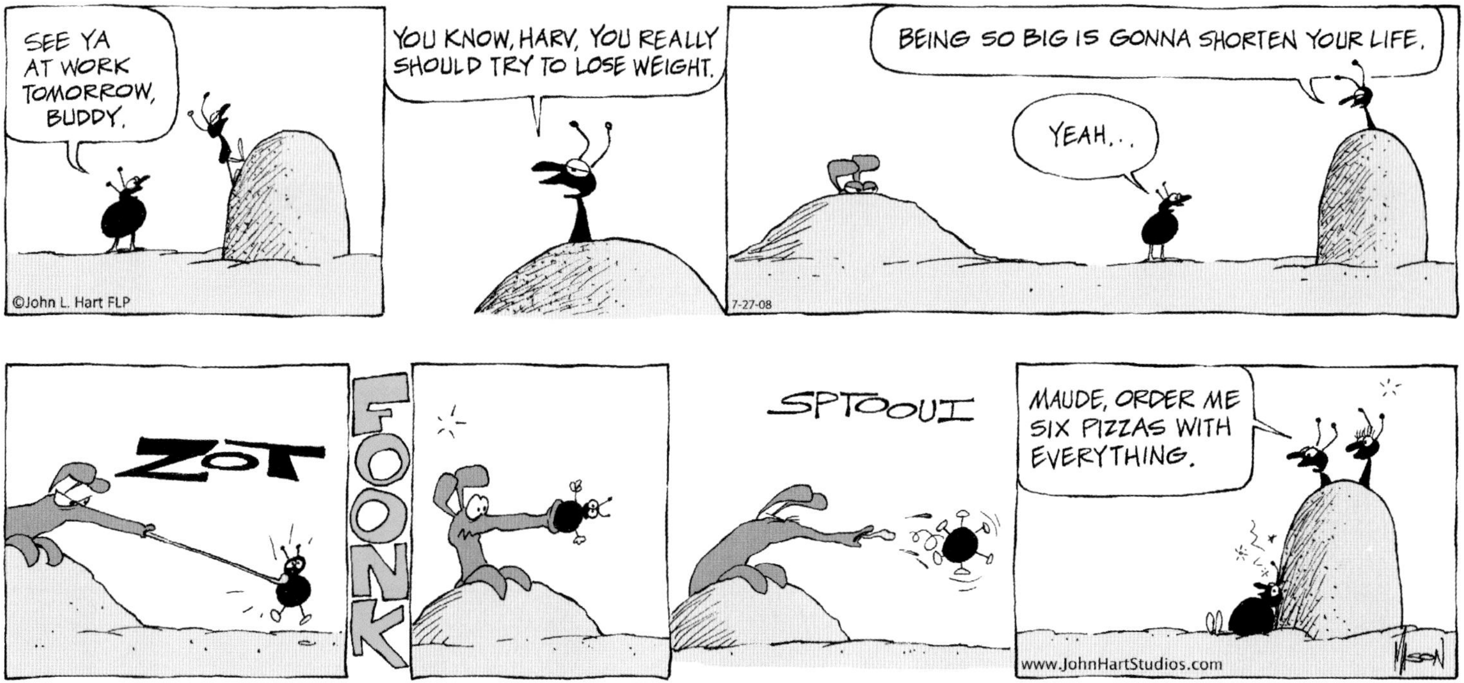
SEE YA AT WORK TOMORROW, BUDDY.
YOU KNOW, HARV, YOU REALLY SHOULD TRY TO LOSE WEIGHT.
BEING SO BIG IS GONNA SHORTEN YOUR LIFE.
YEAH...
©John L. Hart FLP
7-27-08
ZOT
FOONK
SPTOOUI
MAUDE, ORDER ME SIX PIZZAS WITH EVERYTHING.
www.JohnHartStudios.com

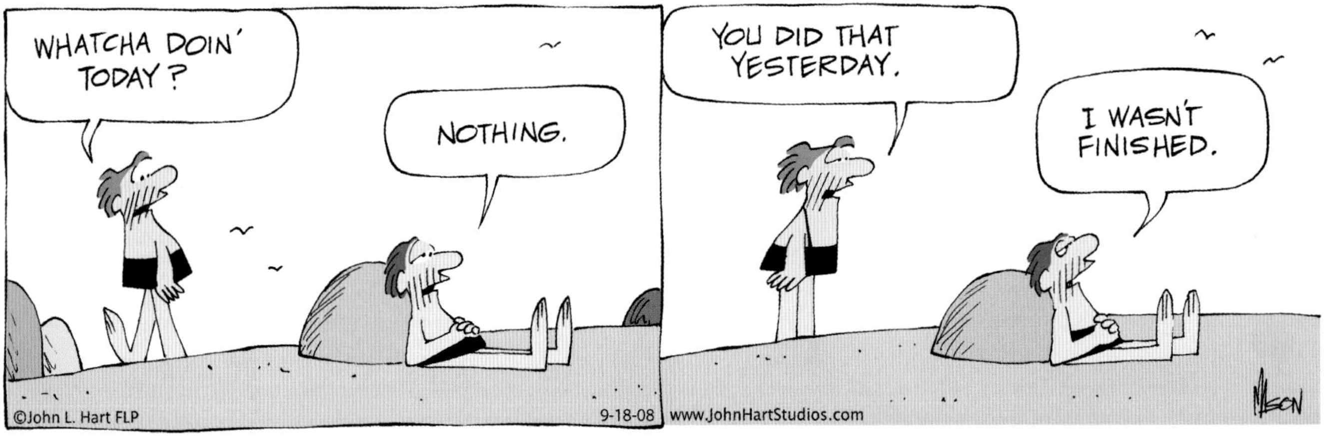
WHATCHA DOIN' TODAY?
NOTHING.
YOU DID THAT YESTERDAY.
I WASN'T FINISHED.
©John L. Hart FLP
9-18-08
www.JohnHartStudios.com
MASON

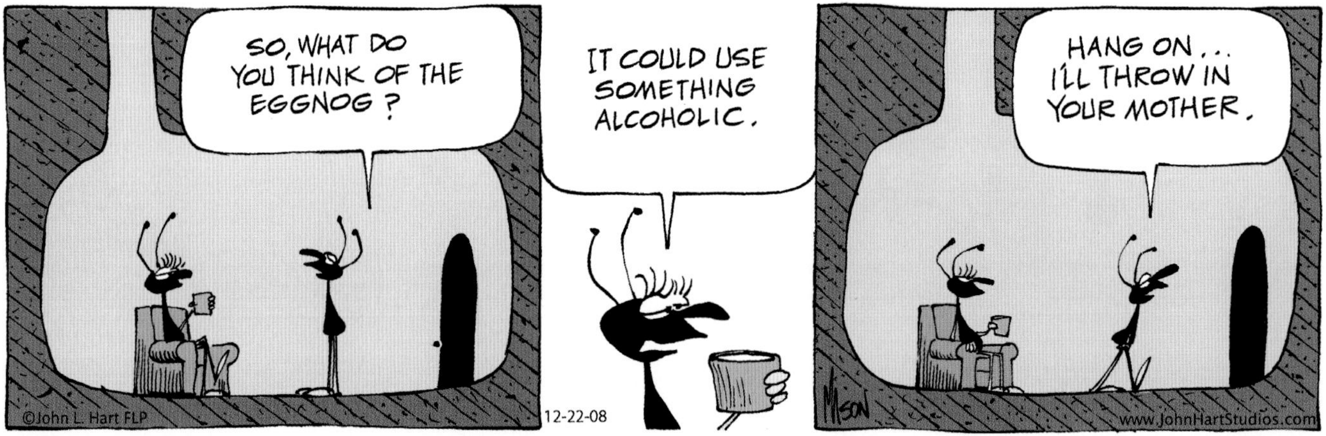
SO, WHAT DO YOU THINK OF THE EGGNOG?
IT COULD USE SOMETHING ALCOHOLIC.
HANG ON... I'LL THROW IN YOUR MOTHER.
©John L. Hart FLP
12-22-08
MASON
www.JohnHartStudios.com

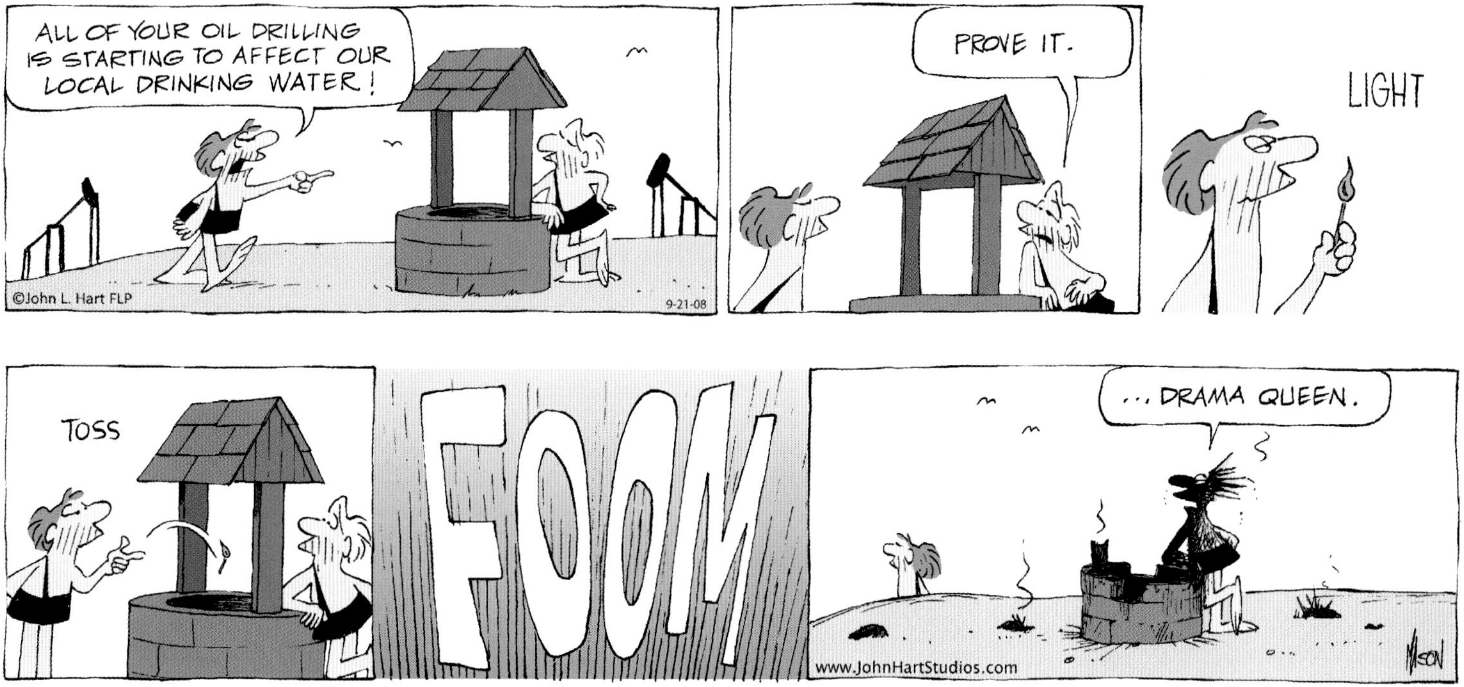
ALL OF YOUR OIL DRILLING IS STARTING TO AFFECT OUR LOCAL DRINKING WATER!
©John L. Hart FLP
9-21-08
PROVE IT.
LIGHT
TOSS
FOOM
...DRAMA QUEEN.
www.JohnHartStudios.com

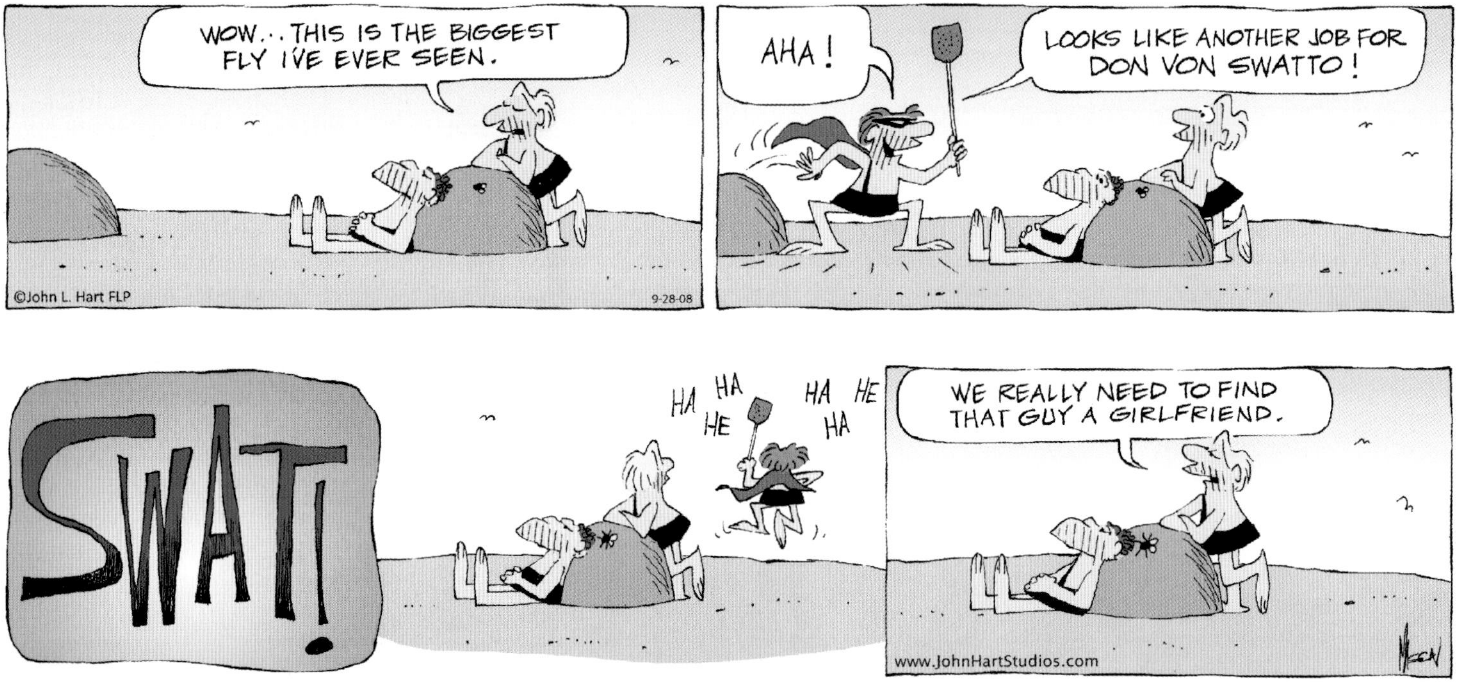
WOW... THIS IS THE BIGGEST FLY I'VE EVER SEEN.
©John L. Hart FLP
9-28-08
AHA!
LOOKS LIKE ANOTHER JOB FOR DON VON SWATTO!
SWAT!
HA HA HE HA HE HA HE HA
WE REALLY NEED TO FIND THAT GUY A GIRLFRIEND.
www.JohnHartStudios.com

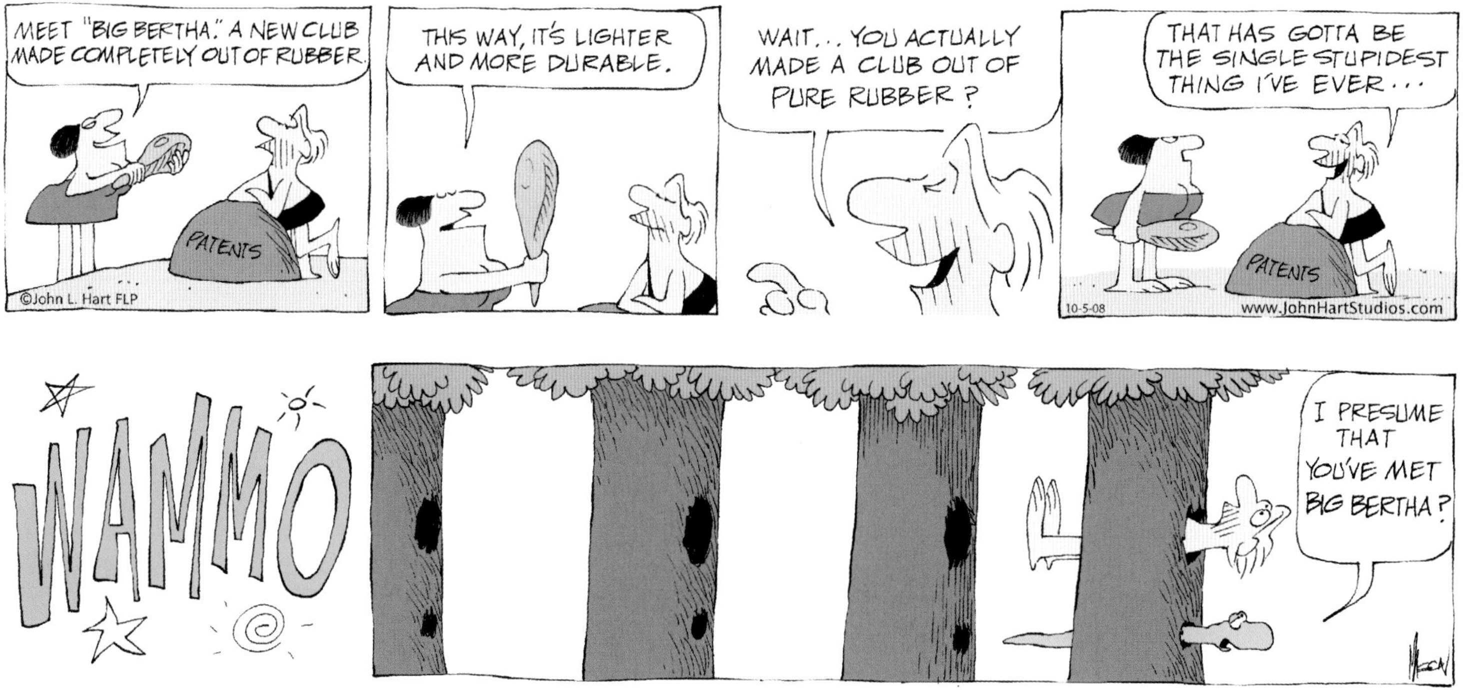
MEET "BIG BERTHA." A NEW CLUB MADE COMPLETELY OUT OF RUBBER.
PATENTS
©John L. Hart FLP
THIS WAY, IT'S LIGHTER AND MORE DURABLE.
WAIT... YOU ACTUALLY MADE A CLUB OUT OF PURE RUBBER?
THAT HAS GOTTA BE THE SINGLE STUPIDEST THING I'VE EVER...
PATENTS
10-5-08
www.JohnHartStudios.com
WAMMO
I PRESUME THAT YOU'VE MET BIG BERTHA?

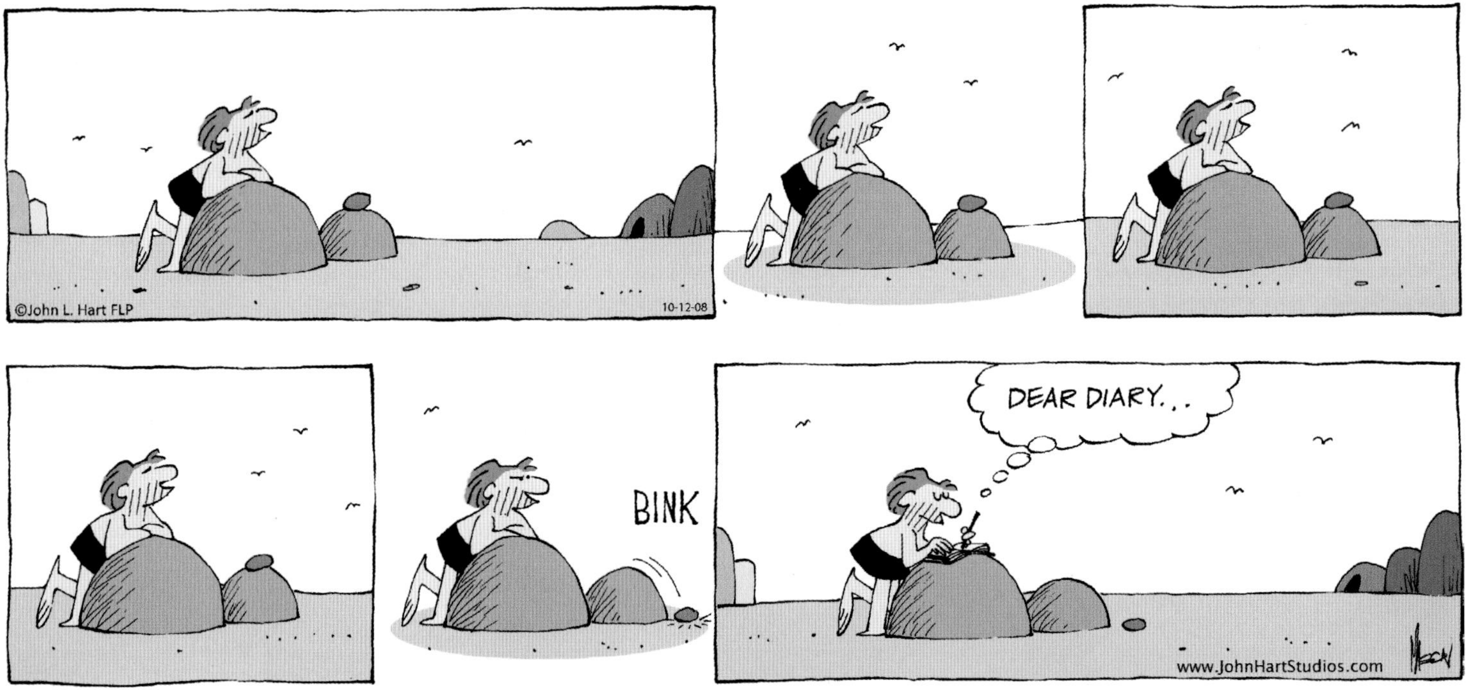
©John L. Hart FLP
10-12-08
BINK
DEAR DIARY...
www.JohnHartStudios.com

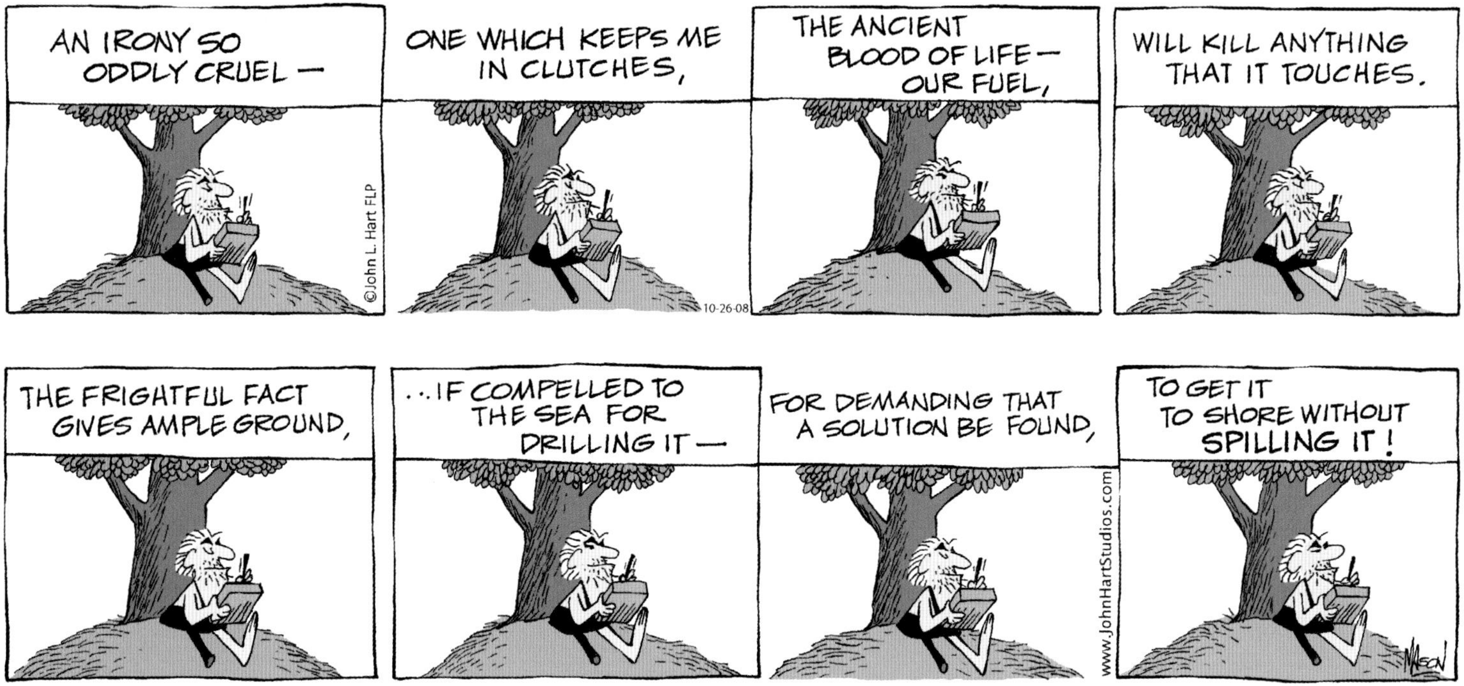
AN IRONY SO ODDLY CRUEL —
©John L. Hart FLP
ONE WHICH KEEPS ME IN CLUTCHES,
10-26-08
THE ANCIENT BLOOD OF LIFE — OUR FUEL,
WILL KILL ANYTHING THAT IT TOUCHES.
THE FRIGHTFUL FACT GIVES AMPLE GROUND,
...IF COMPELLED TO THE SEA FOR DRILLING IT —
FOR DEMANDING THAT A SOLUTION BE FOUND,
www.JohnHartStudios.com
TO GET IT TO SHORE WITHOUT SPILLING IT!
MASON

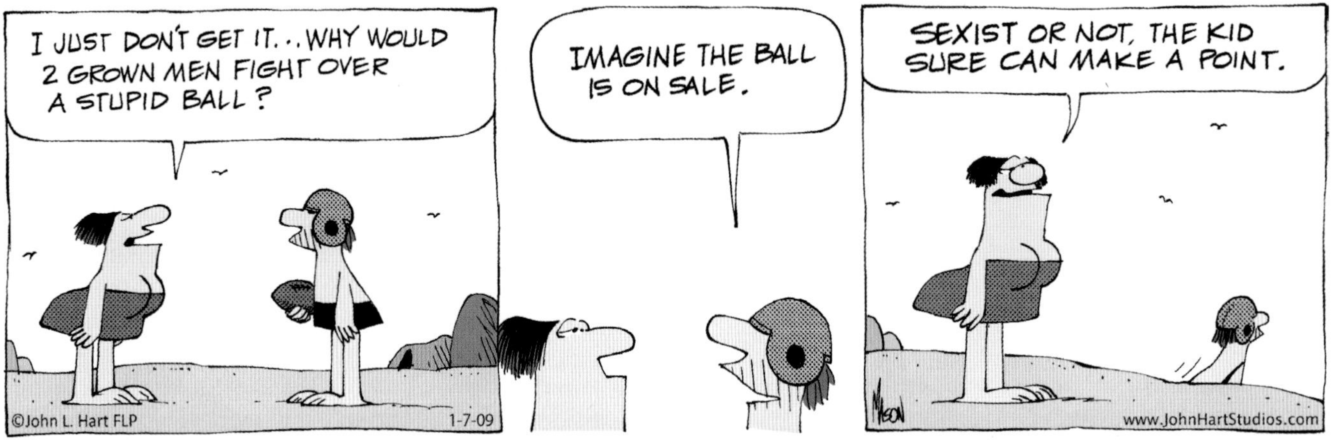
I JUST DON'T GET IT...WHY WOULD 2 GROWN MEN FIGHT OVER A STUPID BALL?
IMAGINE THE BALL IS ON SALE.
SEXIST OR NOT, THE KID SURE CAN MAKE A POINT.
©John L. Hart FLP
1-7-09
www.JohnHartStudios.com

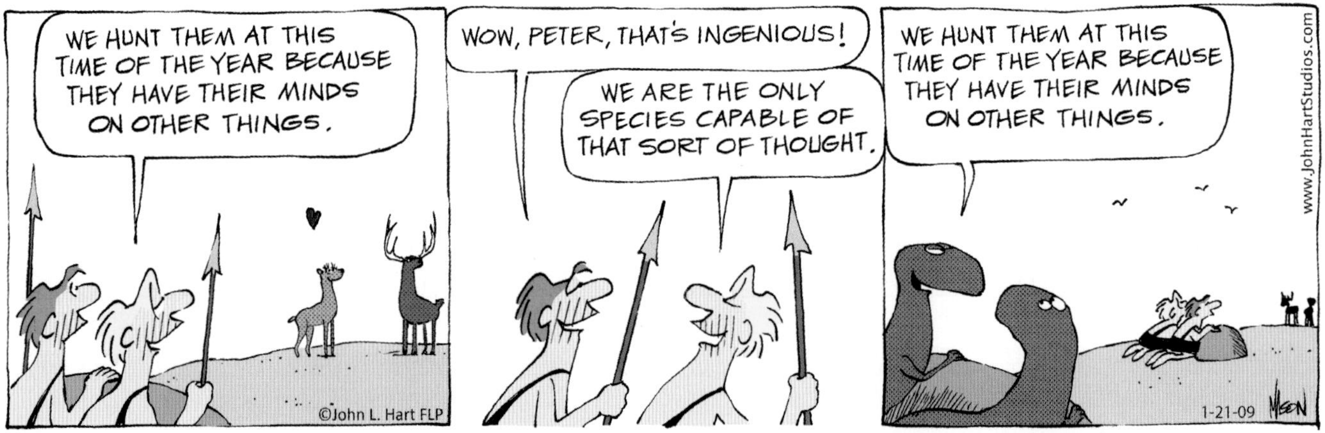
WE HUNT THEM AT THIS TIME OF THE YEAR BECAUSE THEY HAVE THEIR MINDS ON OTHER THINGS.
WOW, PETER, THAT'S INGENIOUS!
WE ARE THE ONLY SPECIES CAPABLE OF THAT SORT OF THOUGHT.
WE HUNT THEM AT THIS TIME OF THE YEAR BECAUSE THEY HAVE THEIR MINDS ON OTHER THINGS.
©John L. Hart FLP
1-21-09
www.JohnHartStudios.com

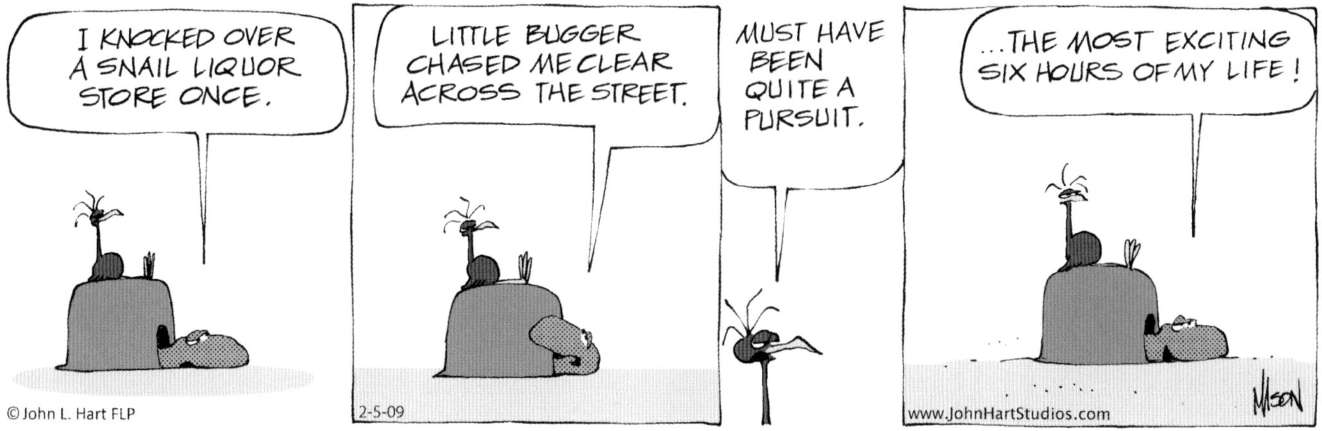
I KNOCKED OVER A SNAIL LIQUOR STORE ONCE.
LITTLE BUGGER CHASED ME CLEAR ACROSS THE STREET.
MUST HAVE BEEN QUITE A PURSUIT.
...THE MOST EXCITING SIX HOURS OF MY LIFE!
© John L. Hart FLP
2-5-09
www.JohnHartStudios.com
MASON

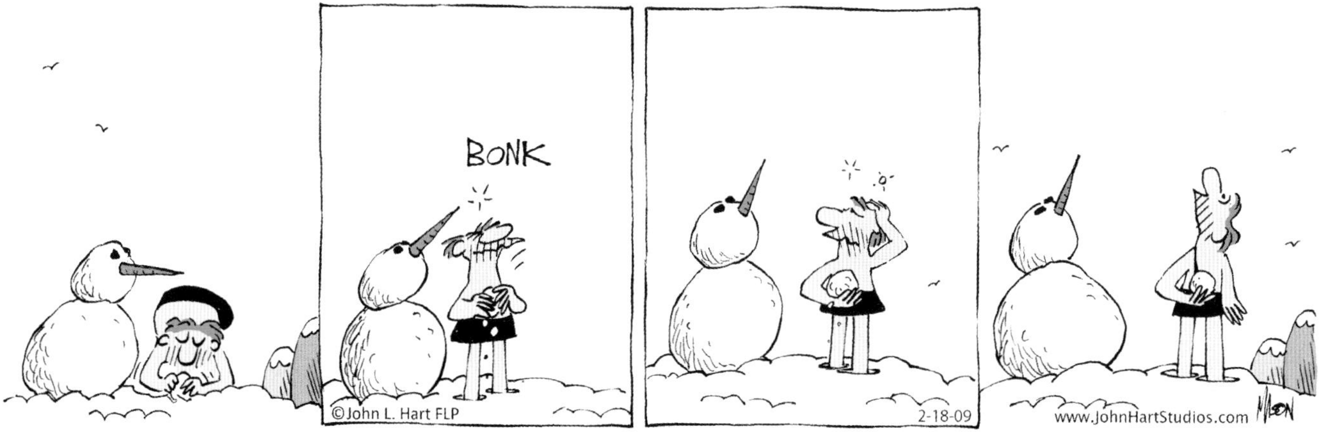
BONK
©John L. Hart FLP
2-18-09
www.JohnHartStudios.com
MASON

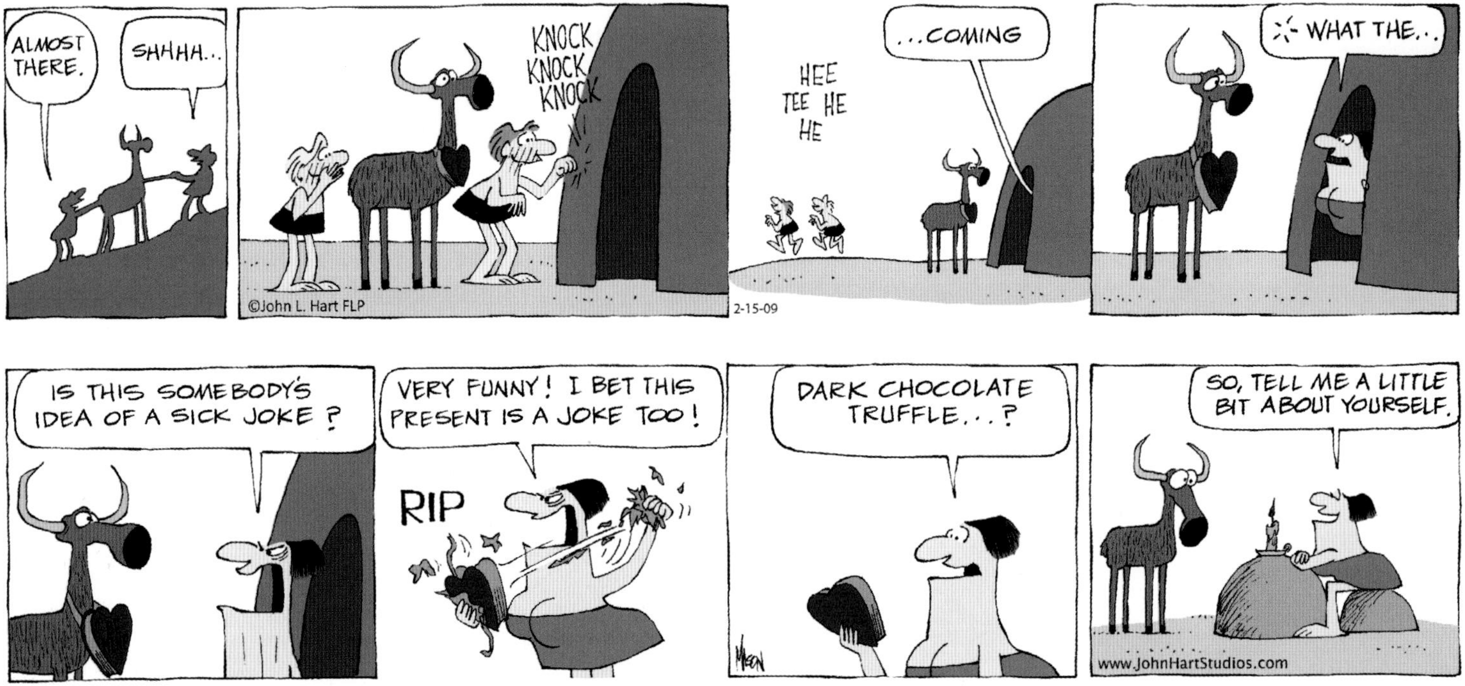
ALMOST THERE.
SHHHH...
KNOCK KNOCK KNOCK
©John L. Hart FLP
HEE TEE HE HE
...COMING
2-15-09
WHAT THE...
IS THIS SOMEBODY'S IDEA OF A SICK JOKE?
VERY FUNNY! I BET THIS PRESENT IS A JOKE TOO!
RIP
DARK CHOCOLATE TRUFFLE...?
SO, TELL ME A LITTLE BIT ABOUT YOURSELF.
www.JohnHartStudios.com

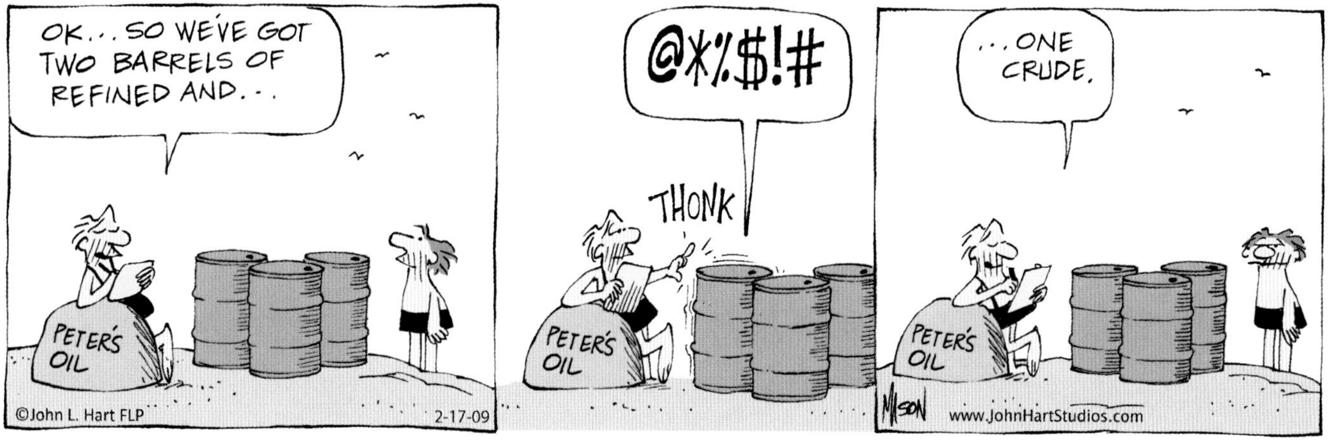
OK... SO WE'VE GOT TWO BARRELS OF REFINED AND...
@*%$!#
THONK
...ONE CRUDE.
©John L. Hart FLP
2-17-09
MASON
www.JohnHartStudios.com

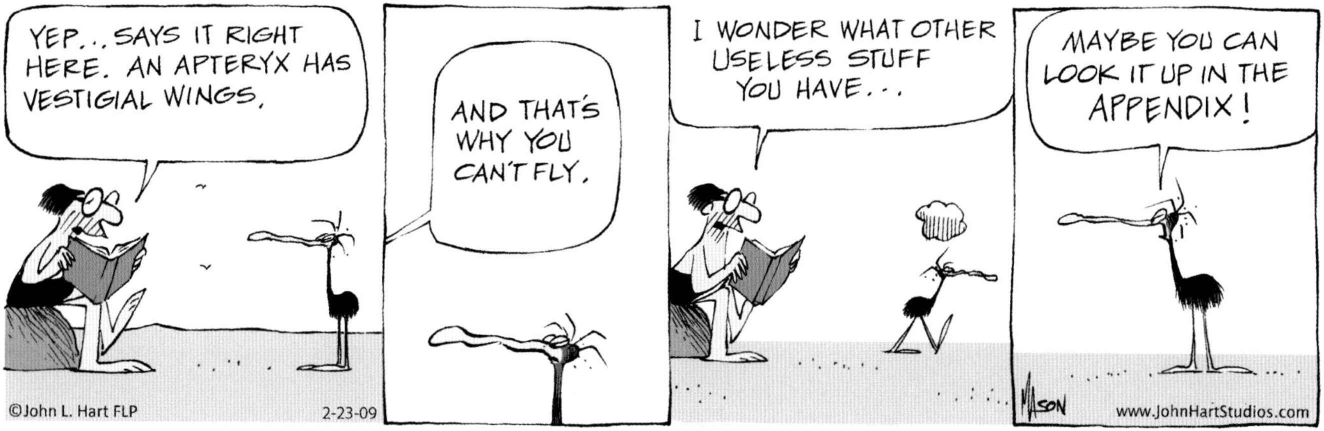
YEP... SAYS IT RIGHT HERE. AN APTERYX HAS VESTIGIAL WINGS.
AND THAT'S WHY YOU CAN'T FLY.
I WONDER WHAT OTHER USELESS STUFF YOU HAVE...
MAYBE YOU CAN LOOK IT UP IN THE APPENDIX!
©John L. Hart FLP
2-23-09
MASON
www.JohnHartStudios.com

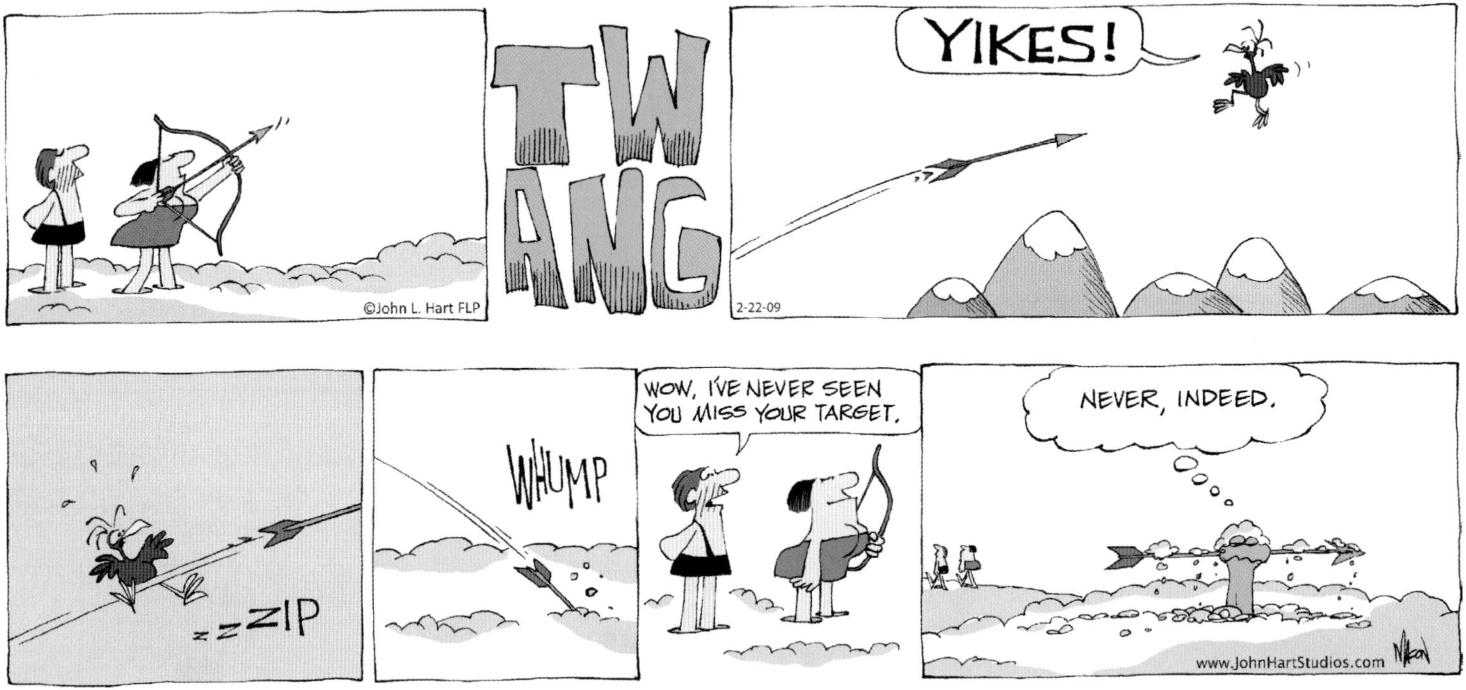
©John L. Hart FLP
TWANG
YIKES!
2-22-09
zzZIP
WHUMP
WOW, I'VE NEVER SEEN YOU MISS YOUR TARGET.
NEVER, INDEED.
www.JohnHartStudios.com

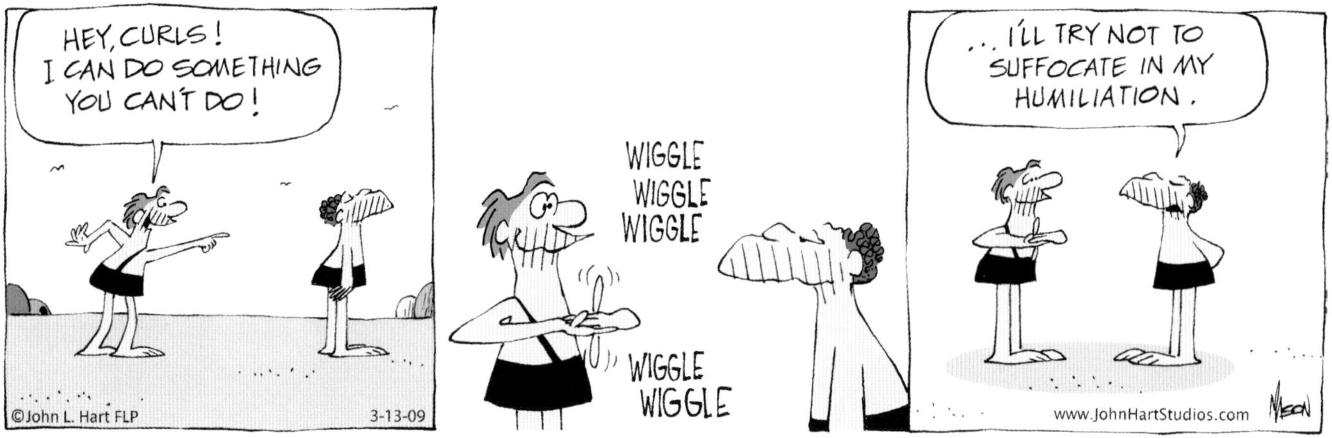
HEY, CURLS! I CAN DO SOMETHING YOU CAN'T DO!
WIGGLE WIGGLE WIGGLE
WIGGLE WIGGLE
...I'LL TRY NOT TO SUFFOCATE IN MY HUMILIATION.
©John L. Hart FLP
3-13-09
www.JohnHartStudios.com
MASON

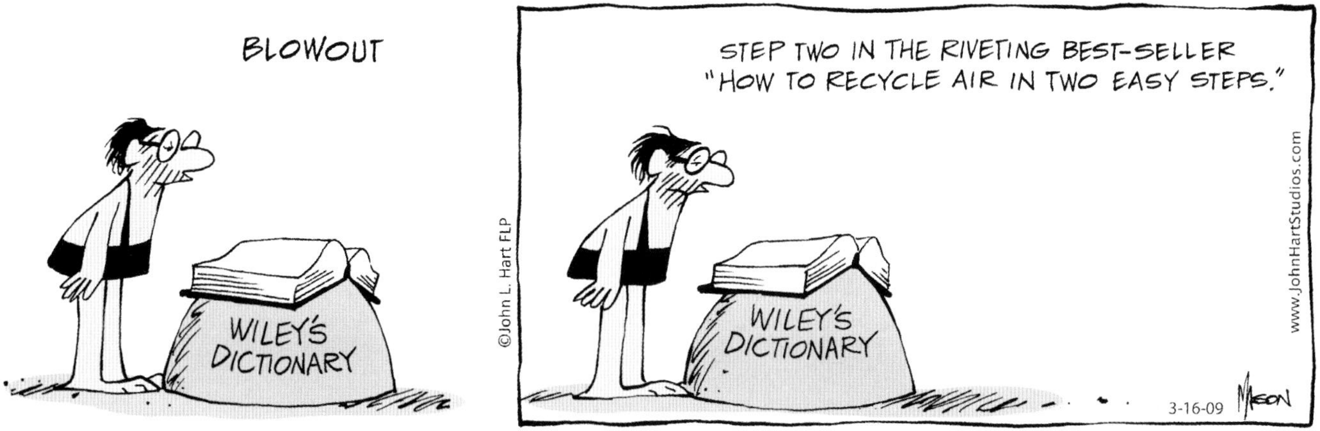
BLOWOUT
WILEY'S DICTIONARY
©John L. Hart FLP
STEP TWO IN THE RIVETING BEST-SELLER "HOW TO RECYCLE AIR IN TWO EASY STEPS."
WILEY'S DICTIONARY
www.JohnHartStudios.com
3-16-09
MASON

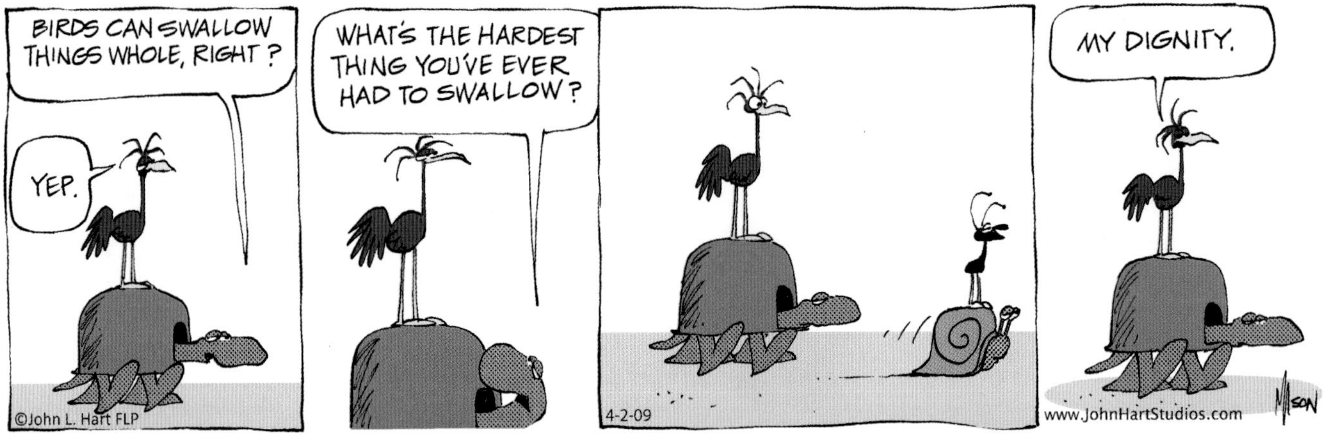
BIRDS CAN SWALLOW THINGS WHOLE, RIGHT?
YEP.
WHAT'S THE HARDEST THING YOU'VE EVER HAD TO SWALLOW?
MY DIGNITY.
©John L. Hart FLP
4-2-09
www.JohnHartStudios.com

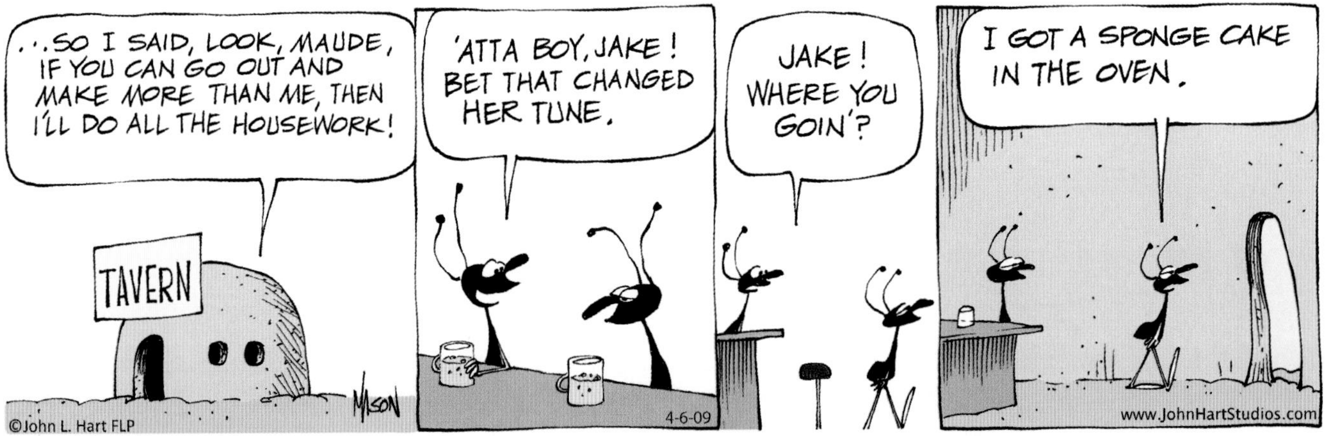
. . .SO I SAID, LOOK, MAUDE, IF YOU CAN GO OUT AND MAKE MORE THAN ME, THEN I'LL DO ALL THE HOUSEWORK!
TAVERN
'ATTA BOY, JAKE! BET THAT CHANGED HER TUNE.
JAKE! WHERE YOU GOIN'?
I GOT A SPONGE CAKE IN THE OVEN.
©John L. Hart FLP
4-6-09
www.JohnHartStudios.com

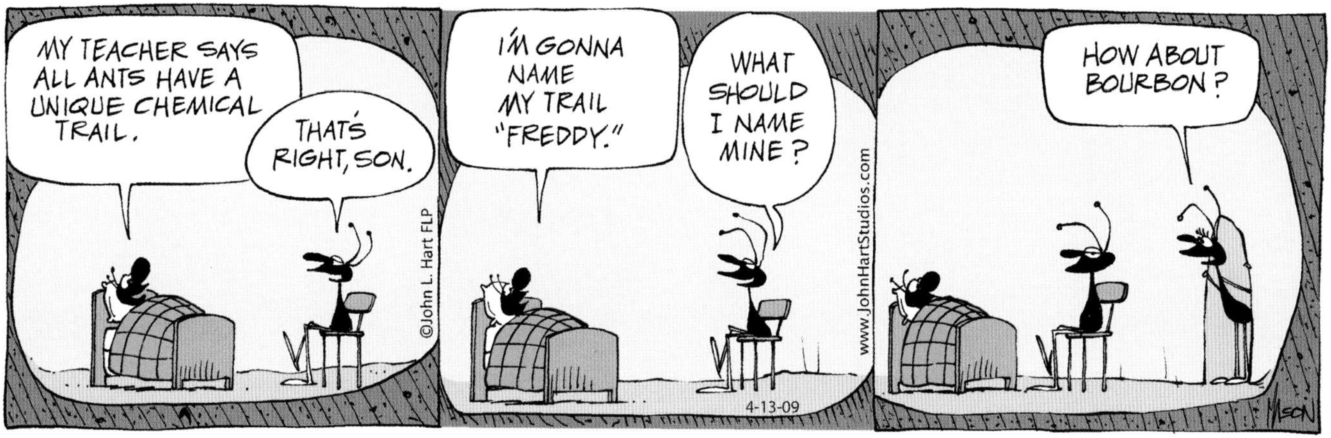
MY TEACHER SAYS ALL ANTS HAVE A UNIQUE CHEMICAL TRAIL.
THAT'S RIGHT, SON.
I'M GONNA NAME MY TRAIL "FREDDY."
WHAT SHOULD I NAME MINE?
HOW ABOUT BOURBON?
©John L. Hart FLP
www.JohnHartStudios.com
4-13-09

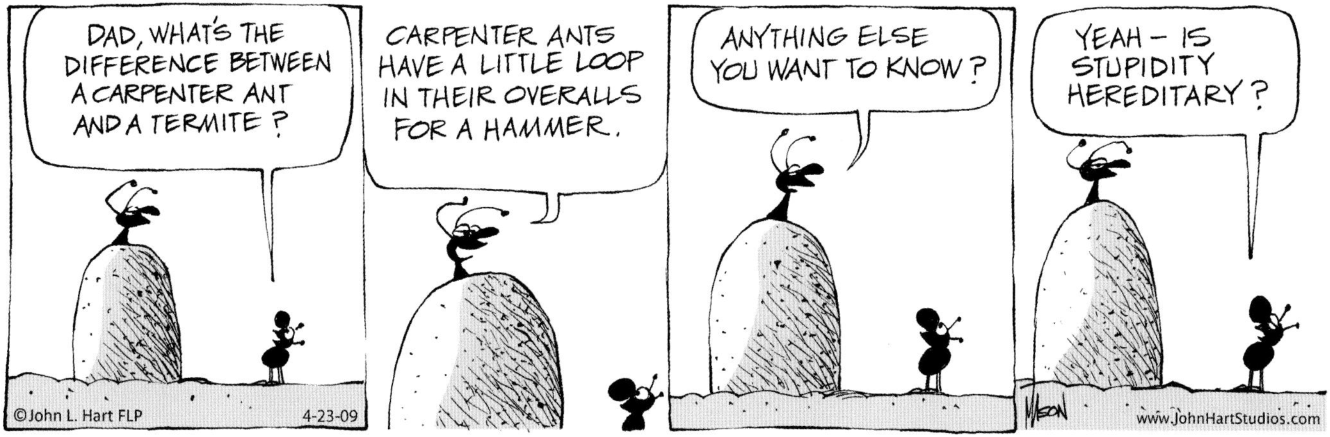
DAD, WHAT'S THE DIFFERENCE BETWEEN A CARPENTER ANT AND A TERMITE?
CARPENTER ANTS HAVE A LITTLE LOOP IN THEIR OVERALLS FOR A HAMMER.
ANYTHING ELSE YOU WANT TO KNOW?
YEAH – IS STUPIDITY HEREDITARY?
©John L. Hart FLP
4-23-09
www.JohnHartStudios.com

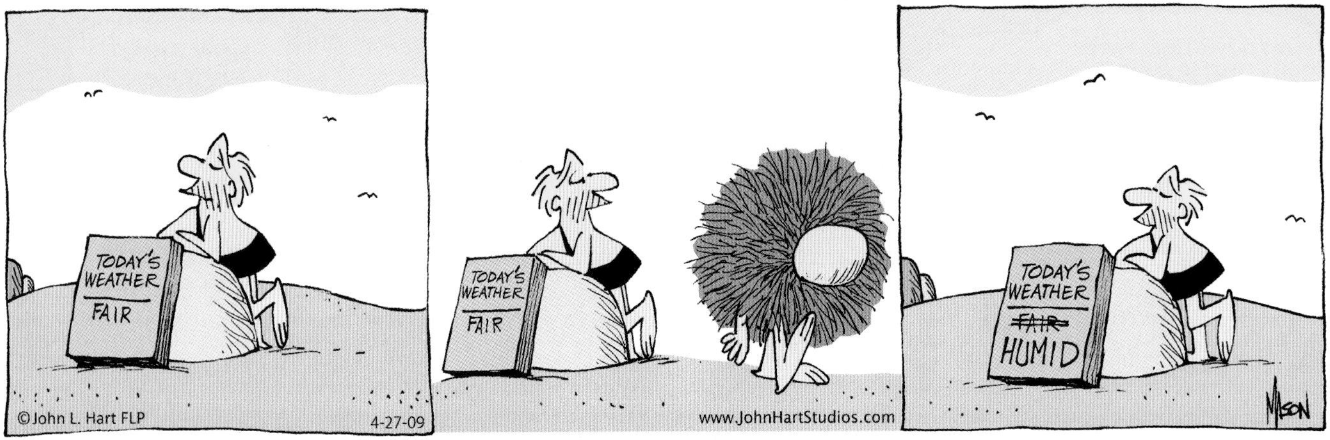
TODAY'S WEATHER
FAIR
TODAY'S WEATHER
FAIR
TODAY'S WEATHER
~~FAIR~~
HUMID
©John L. Hart FLP
4-27-09
www.JohnHartStudios.com
MASON

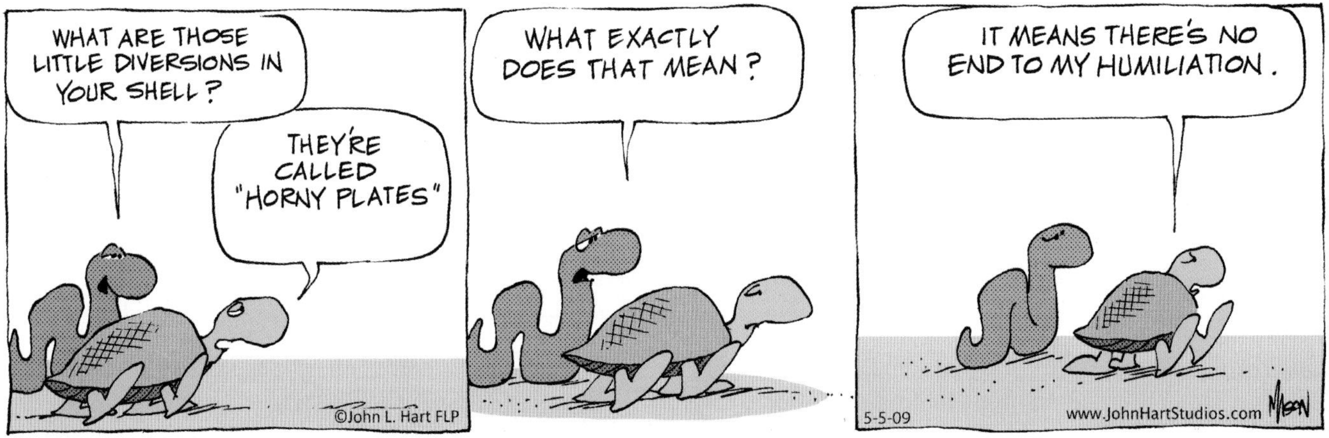
WHAT ARE THOSE LITTLE DIVERSIONS IN YOUR SHELL?
THEY'RE CALLED "HORNY PLATES"
©John L. Hart FLP
WHAT EXACTLY DOES THAT MEAN?
IT MEANS THERE'S NO END TO MY HUMILIATION.
5-5-09
www.JohnHartStudios.com
MASON

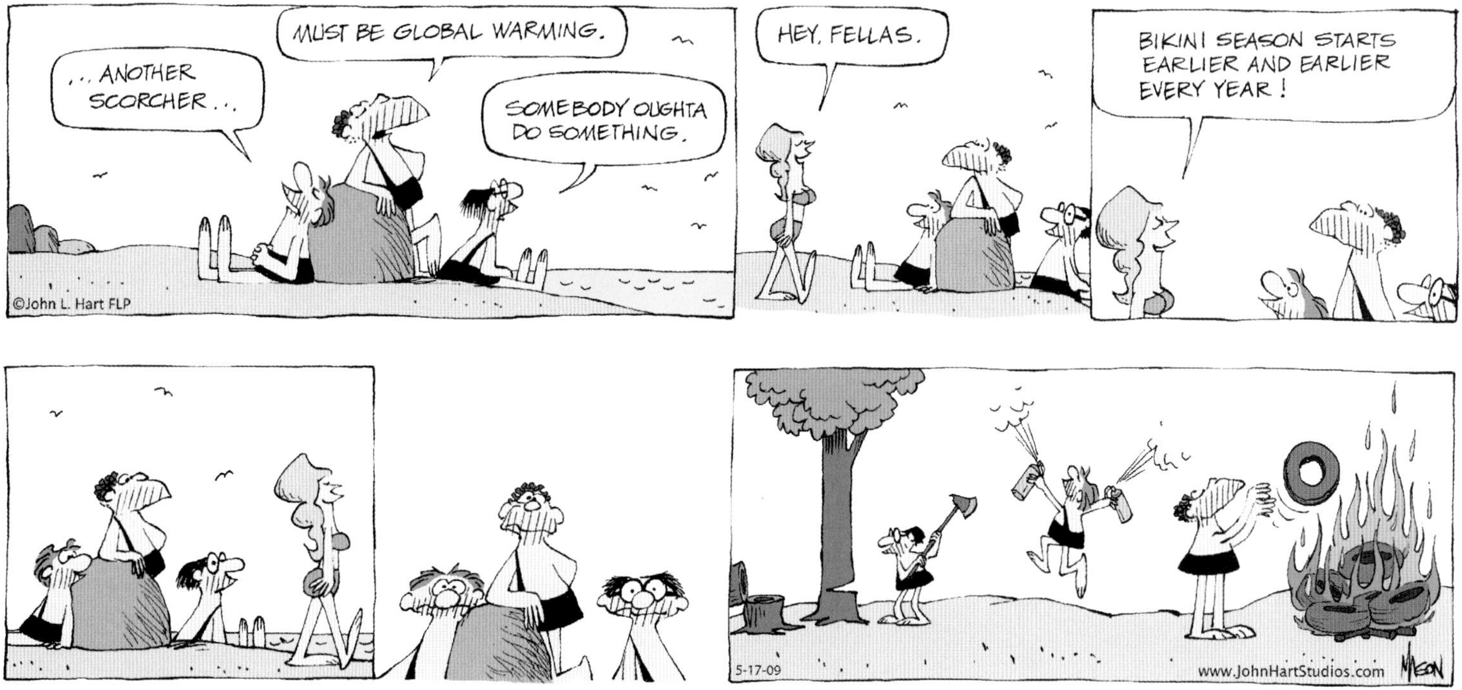
. . . ANOTHER SCORCHER . . .
MUST BE GLOBAL WARMING.
SOMEBODY OUGHTA DO SOMETHING.
HEY, FELLAS.
BIKINI SEASON STARTS EARLIER AND EARLIER EVERY YEAR!
©John L. Hart FLP
5-17-09
www.JohnHartStudios.com
MASON

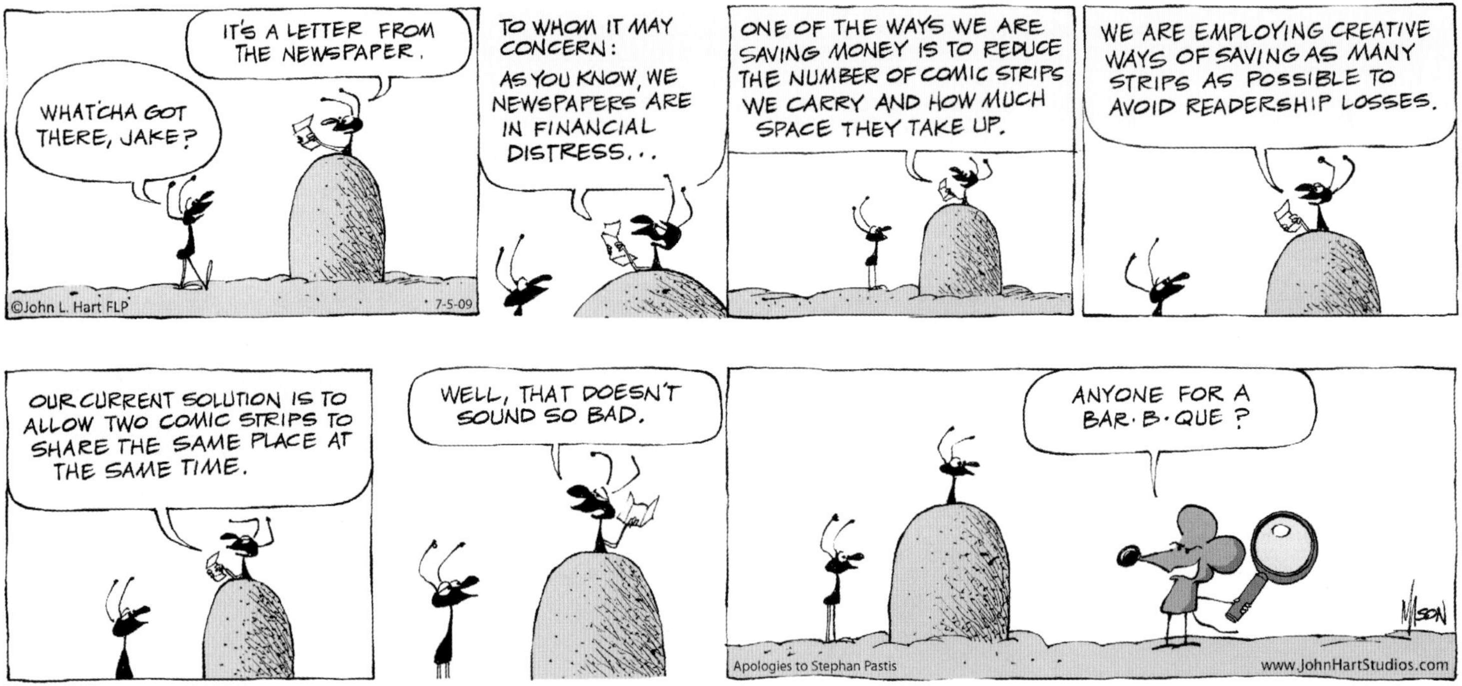
WHAT'CHA GOT THERE, JAKE?
IT'S A LETTER FROM THE NEWSPAPER.
©John L. Hart FLP
7-5-09
TO WHOM IT MAY CONCERN:
AS YOU KNOW, WE NEWSPAPERS ARE IN FINANCIAL DISTRESS...
ONE OF THE WAYS WE ARE SAVING MONEY IS TO REDUCE THE NUMBER OF COMIC STRIPS WE CARRY AND HOW MUCH SPACE THEY TAKE UP.
WE ARE EMPLOYING CREATIVE WAYS OF SAVING AS MANY STRIPS AS POSSIBLE TO AVOID READERSHIP LOSSES.
OUR CURRENT SOLUTION IS TO ALLOW TWO COMIC STRIPS TO SHARE THE SAME PLACE AT THE SAME TIME.
WELL, THAT DOESN'T SOUND SO BAD.
ANYONE FOR A BAR·B·QUE?
Apologies to Stephan Pastis
www.JohnHartStudios.com

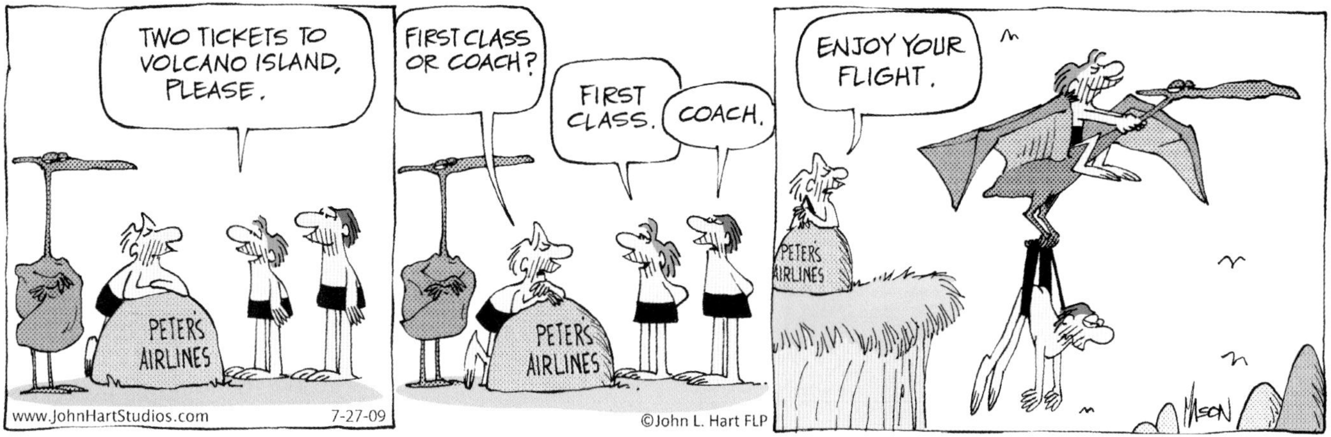
TWO TICKETS TO VOLCANO ISLAND, PLEASE.
PETER'S AIRLINES
FIRST CLASS OR COACH?
FIRST CLASS.
COACH.
PETER'S AIRLINES
ENJOY YOUR FLIGHT.
PETER'S AIRLINES
www.JohnHartStudios.com
7-27-09
©John L. Hart FLP
MASON

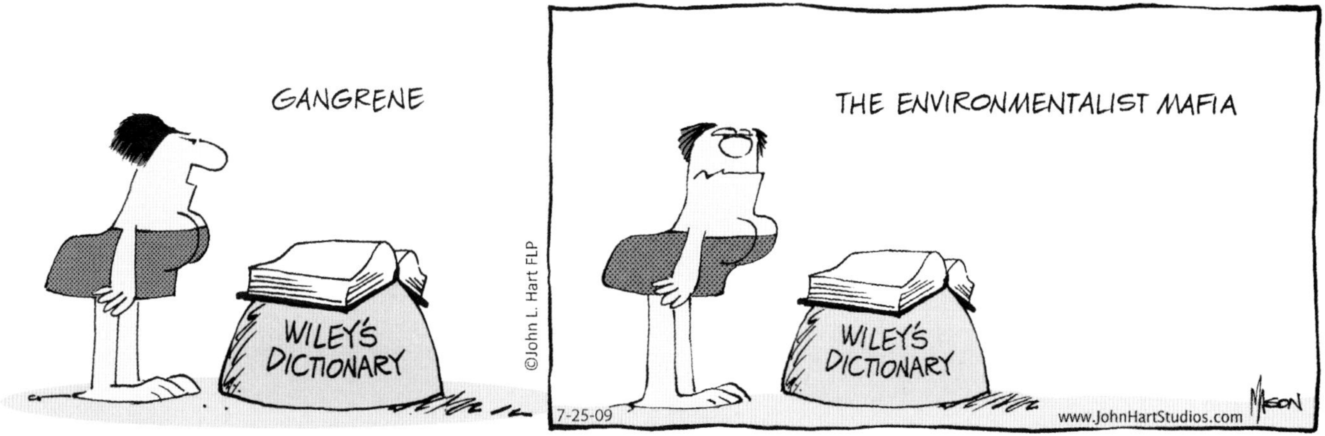
GANGRENE
WILEY'S DICTIONARY
©John L. Hart FLP
THE ENVIRONMENTALIST MAFIA
WILEY'S DICTIONARY
7-25-09
www.JohnHartStudios.com
MASON

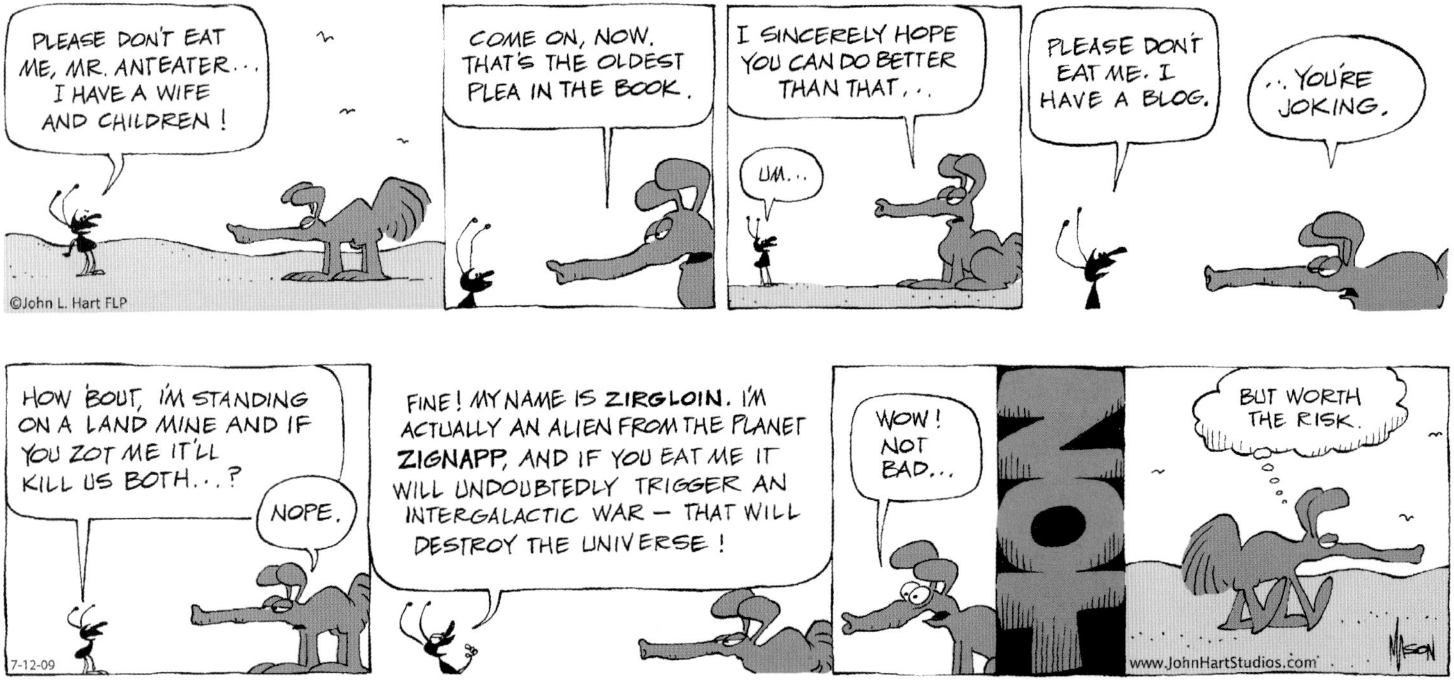

PLEASE DON'T EAT ME, MR. ANTEATER... I HAVE A WIFE AND CHILDREN!
COME ON, NOW. THAT'S THE OLDEST PLEA IN THE BOOK.
I SINCERELY HOPE YOU CAN DO BETTER THAN THAT...
UM...
PLEASE DON'T EAT ME. I HAVE A BLOG.
...YOU'RE JOKING.
HOW 'BOUT, I'M STANDING ON A LAND MINE AND IF YOU ZOT ME IT'LL KILL US BOTH...?
NOPE.
FINE! MY NAME IS ZIRGLOIN. I'M ACTUALLY AN ALIEN FROM THE PLANET ZIGNAPP, AND IF YOU EAT ME IT WILL UNDOUBTEDLY TRIGGER AN INTERGALACTIC WAR — THAT WILL DESTROY THE UNIVERSE!
WOW! NOT BAD...
ZOT
BUT WORTH THE RISK.
©John L. Hart FLP
7-12-09
www.JohnHartStudios.com
MASON

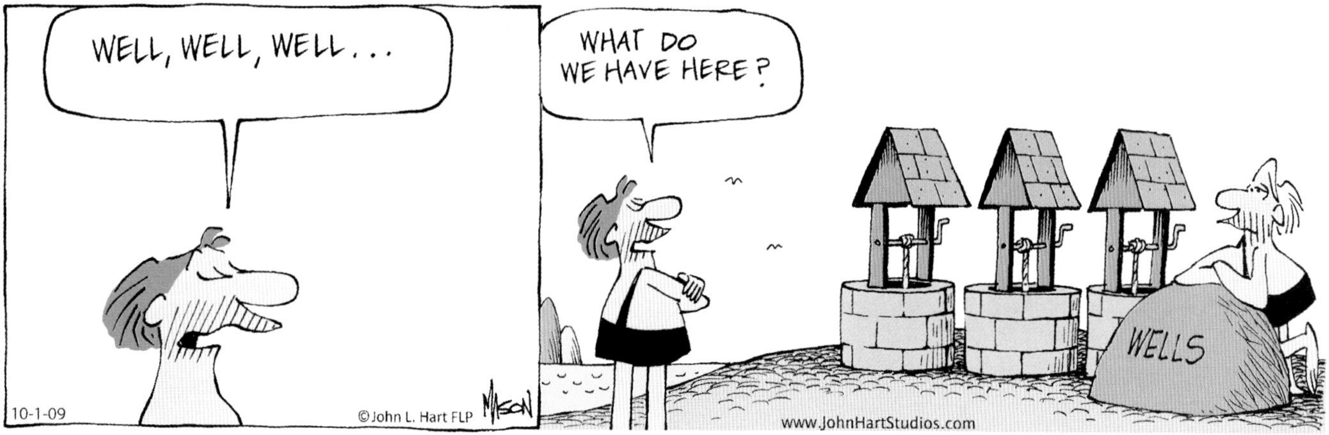

WELL, WELL, WELL...
WHAT DO WE HAVE HERE?
WELLS
10-1-09
©John L. Hart FLP
MASON
www.JohnHartStudios.com

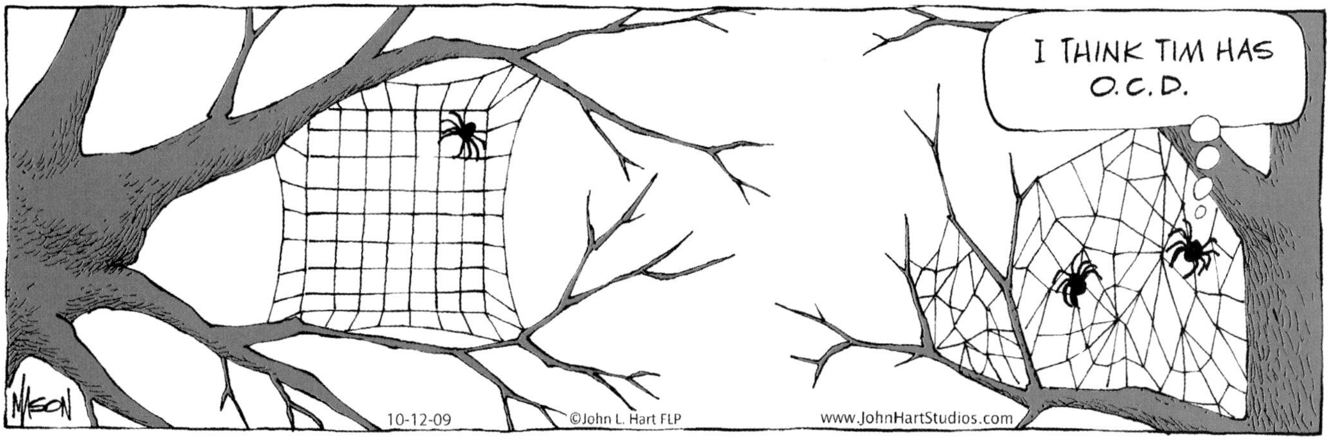

I THINK TIM HAS O.C.D.
MASON
10-12-09
©John L. Hart FLP
www.JohnHartStudios.com

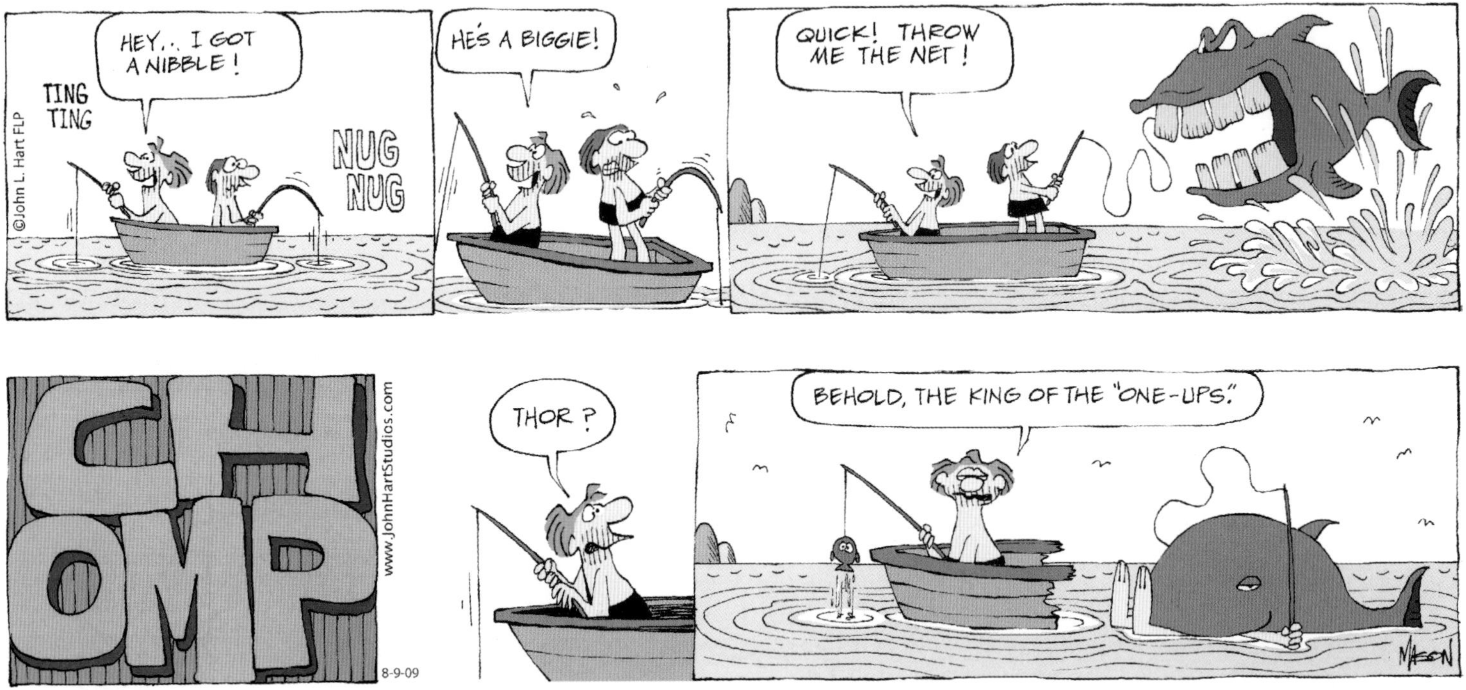
©John L. Hart FLP
TING TING
HEY... I GOT A NIBBLE!
NUG NUG
HE'S A BIGGIE!
QUICK! THROW ME THE NET!
CH OMP
www.JohnHartStudios.com
8-9-09
THOR?
BEHOLD, THE KING OF THE "ONE-UPS."
MASON

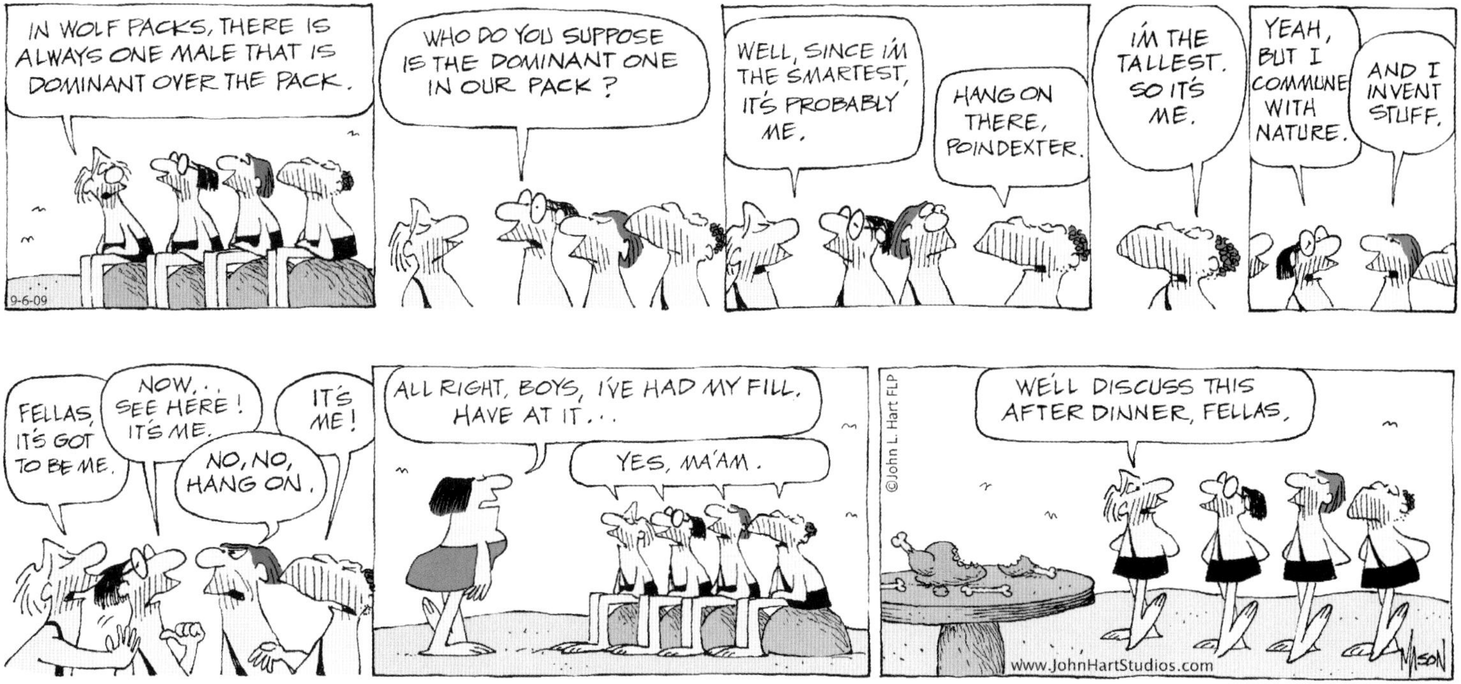
9-6-09
IN WOLF PACKS, THERE IS ALWAYS ONE MALE THAT IS DOMINANT OVER THE PACK.
WHO DO YOU SUPPOSE IS THE DOMINANT ONE IN OUR PACK ?
WELL, SINCE I'M THE SMARTEST, IT'S PROBABLY ME.
HANG ON THERE, POINDEXTER.
I'M THE TALLEST. SO IT'S ME.
YEAH, BUT I COMMUNE WITH NATURE.
AND I INVENT STUFF.
FELLAS, IT'S GOT TO BE ME.
NOW. . . SEE HERE ! IT'S ME.
NO, NO, HANG ON.
IT'S ME !
ALL RIGHT, BOYS, I'VE HAD MY FILL. HAVE AT IT . . .
YES, MA'AM.
©John L. Hart FLP
WE'LL DISCUSS THIS AFTER DINNER, FELLAS.
MASON
www.JohnHartStudios.com

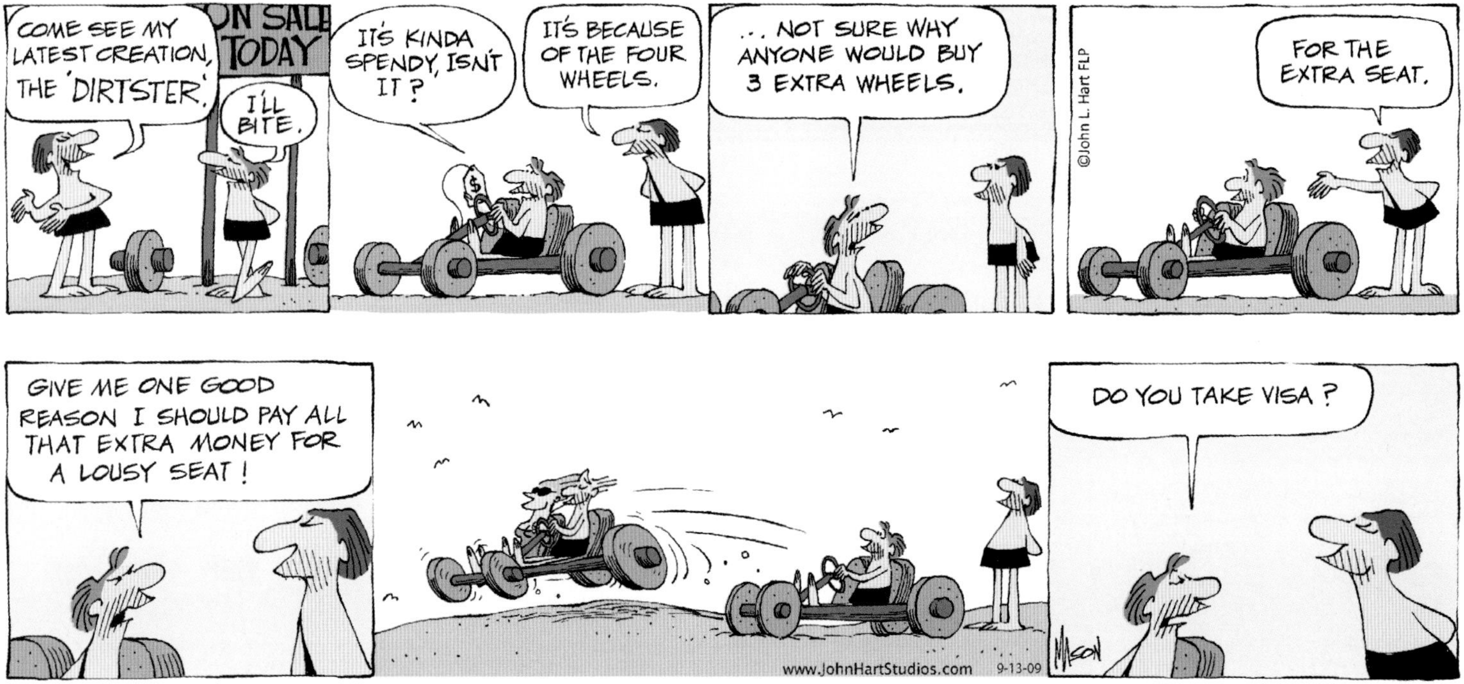
ON SALE TODAY
COME SEE MY LATEST CREATION, THE 'DIRTSTER'.
I'LL BITE.
IT'S KINDA SPENDY, ISN'T IT ?
IT'S BECAUSE OF THE FOUR WHEELS.
... NOT SURE WHY ANYONE WOULD BUY 3 EXTRA WHEELS.
©John L. Hart FLP
FOR THE EXTRA SEAT.
GIVE ME ONE GOOD REASON I SHOULD PAY ALL THAT EXTRA MONEY FOR A LOUSY SEAT !
www.JohnHartStudios.com
9-13-09
MASON
DO YOU TAKE VISA ?

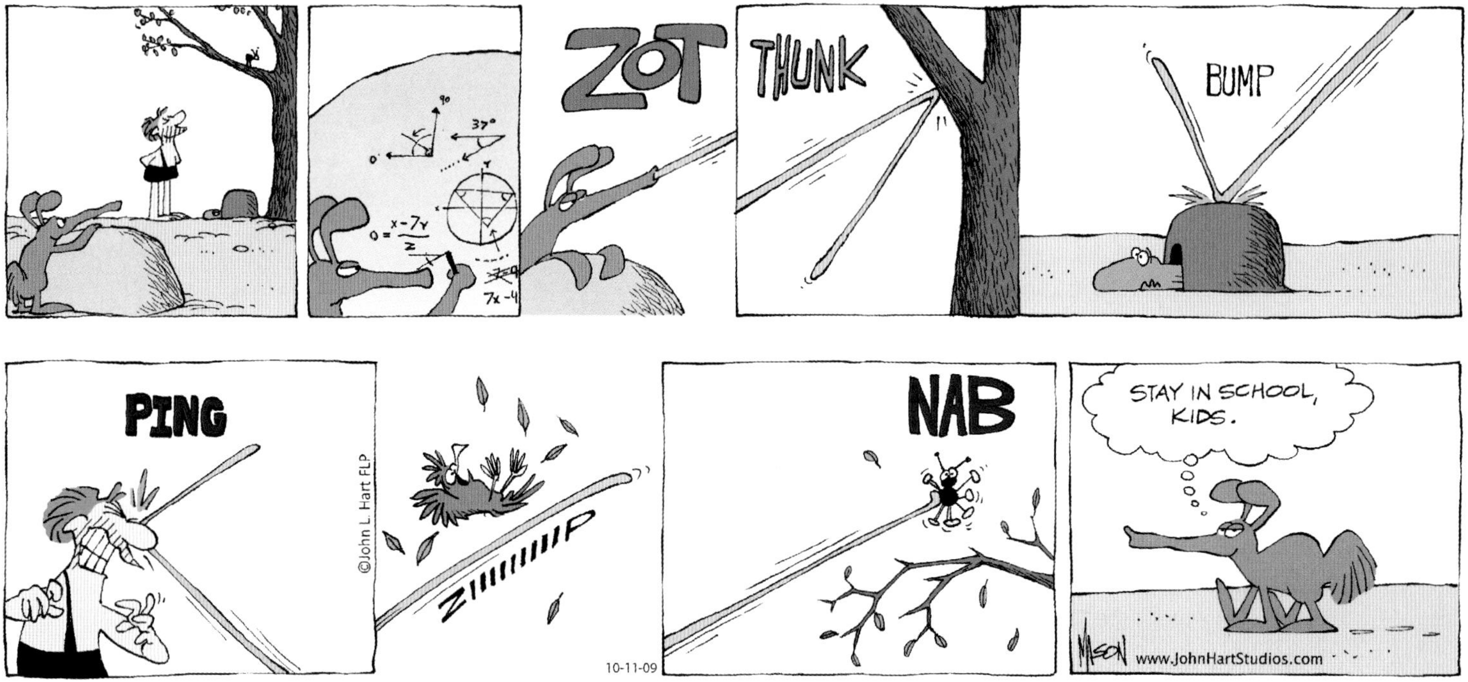

37°
0 = x − 7y / z
7x − 4
ZOT
THUNK
BUMP
PING
©John L. Hart FLP
ZIIIIIIIP
10-11-09
NAB
STAY IN SCHOOL, KIDS.
MASON
www.JohnHartStudios.com

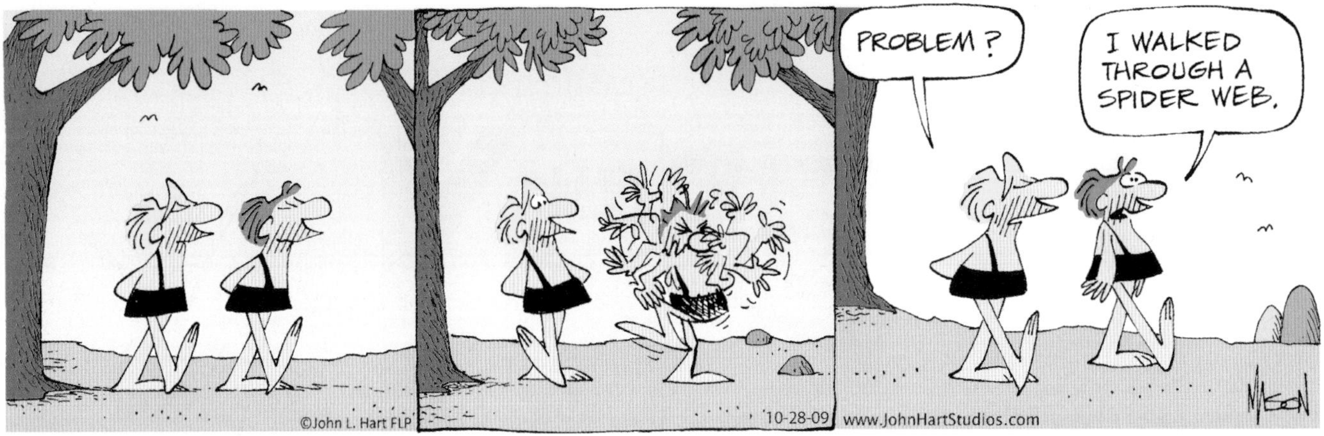
PROBLEM ?
I WALKED THROUGH A SPIDER WEB.
©John L. Hart FLP
10-28-09
www.JohnHartStudios.com
MASON

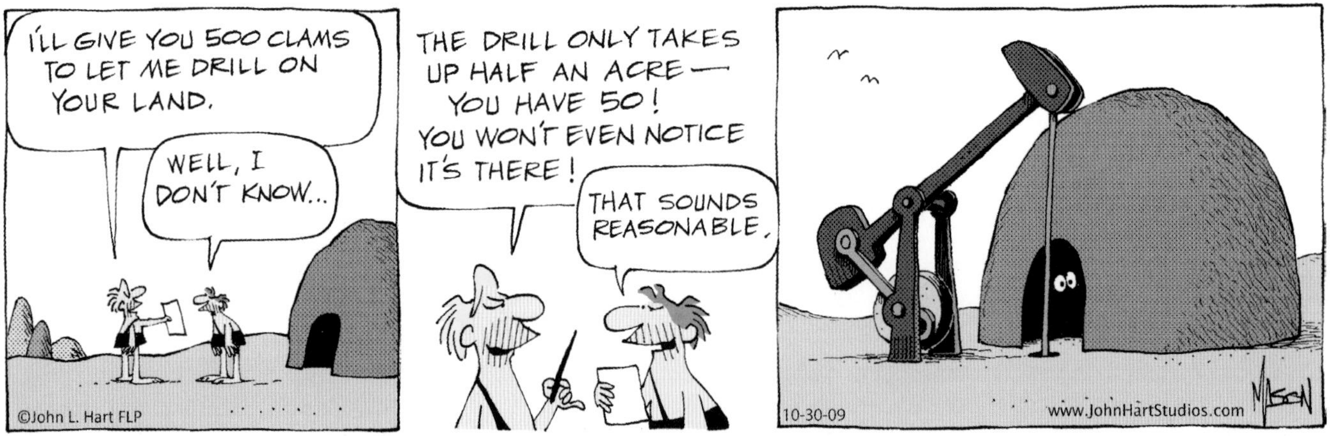
I'LL GIVE YOU 500 CLAMS TO LET ME DRILL ON YOUR LAND.
WELL, I DON'T KNOW...
THE DRILL ONLY TAKES UP HALF AN ACRE— YOU HAVE 50! YOU WON'T EVEN NOTICE IT'S THERE!
THAT SOUNDS REASONABLE.
©John L. Hart FLP
10-30-09
www.JohnHartStudios.com
MASON

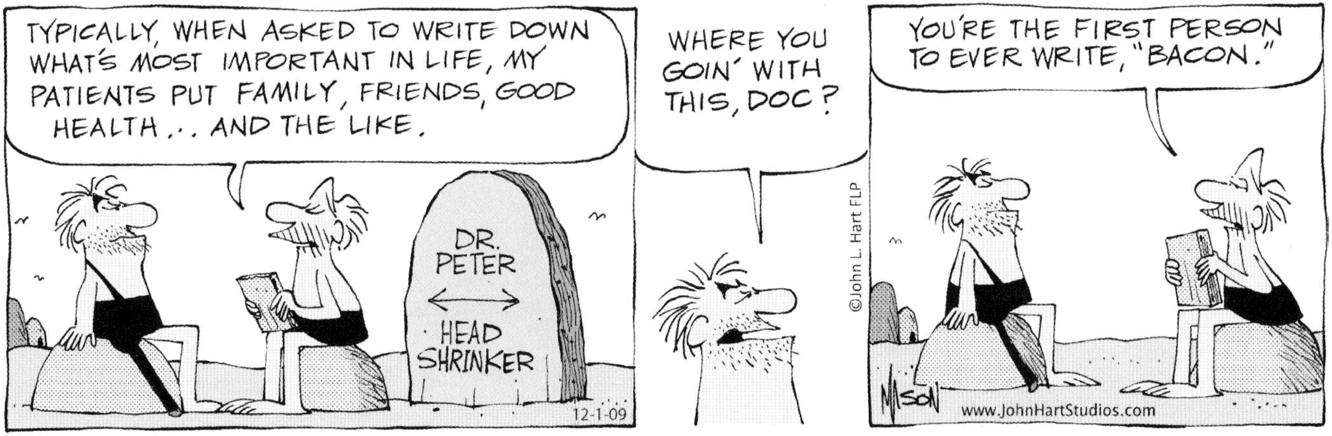
TYPICALLY, WHEN ASKED TO WRITE DOWN WHAT'S MOST IMPORTANT IN LIFE, MY PATIENTS PUT FAMILY, FRIENDS, GOOD HEALTH . . . AND THE LIKE.
DR. PETER
HEAD SHRINKER
12-1-09
WHERE YOU GOIN' WITH THIS, DOC?
©John L. Hart FLP
YOU'RE THE FIRST PERSON TO EVER WRITE, "BACON."
MASON
www.JohnHartStudios.com

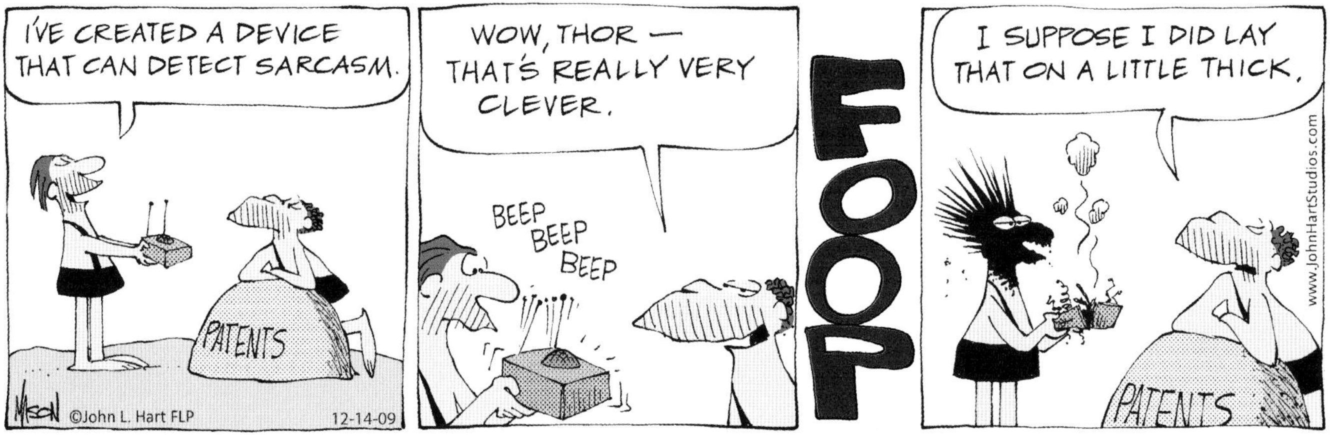
I'VE CREATED A DEVICE THAT CAN DETECT SARCASM.
PATENTS
MASON ©John L. Hart FLP
12-14-09
WOW, THOR — THAT'S REALLY VERY CLEVER.
BEEP
BEEP
BEEP
FOOP
I SUPPOSE I DID LAY THAT ON A LITTLE THICK.
PATENTS
www.JohnHartStudios.com

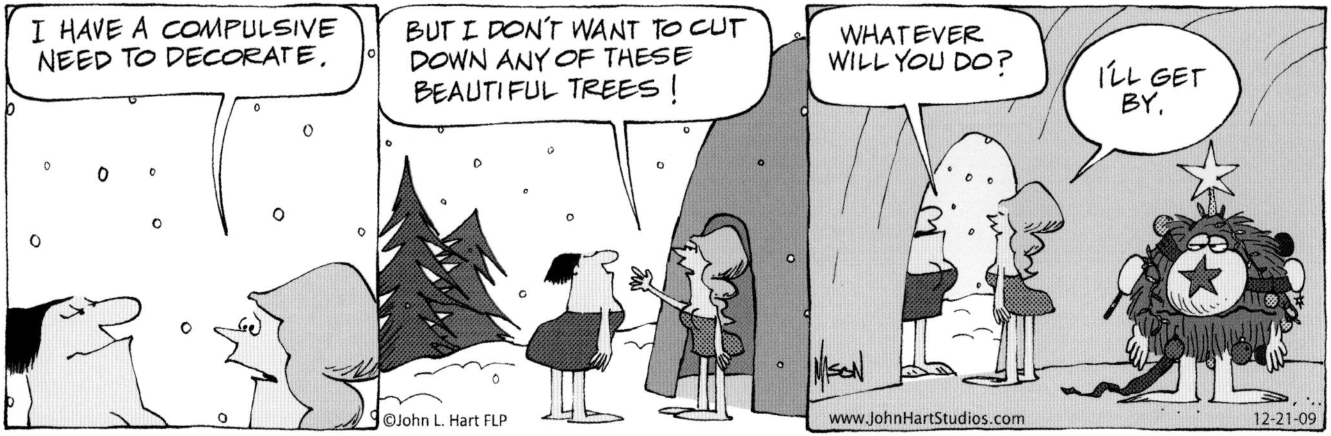
I HAVE A COMPULSIVE NEED TO DECORATE.
BUT I DON'T WANT TO CUT DOWN ANY OF THESE BEAUTIFUL TREES!
WHATEVER WILL YOU DO?
I'LL GET BY.
©John L. Hart FLP
www.JohnHartStudios.com
12-21-09

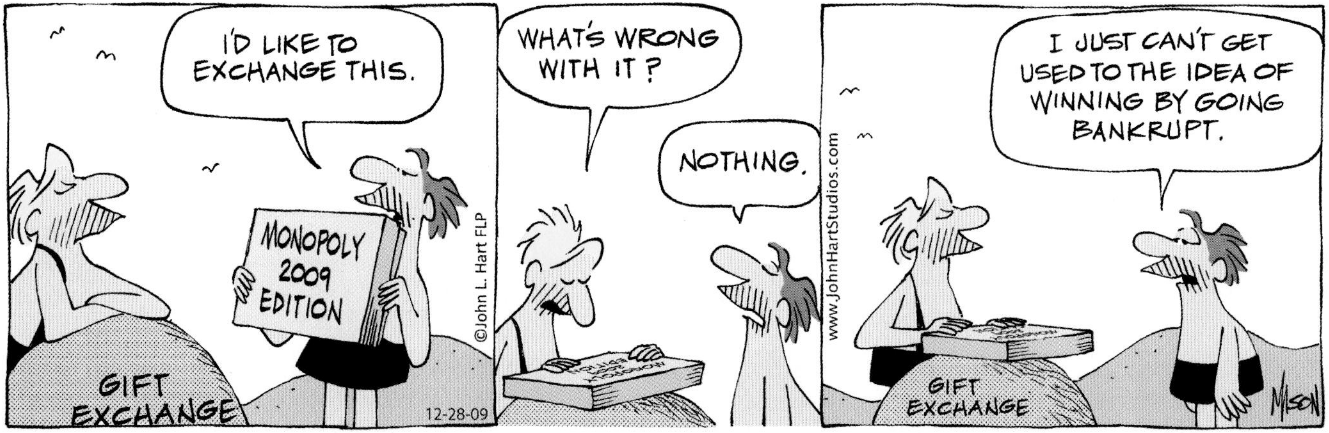
I'D LIKE TO EXCHANGE THIS.
MONOPOLY 2009 EDITION
GIFT EXCHANGE
©John L. Hart FLP
12-28-09
WHAT'S WRONG WITH IT?
NOTHING.
www.JohnHartStudios.com
I JUST CAN'T GET USED TO THE IDEA OF WINNING BY GOING BANKRUPT.
GIFT EXCHANGE

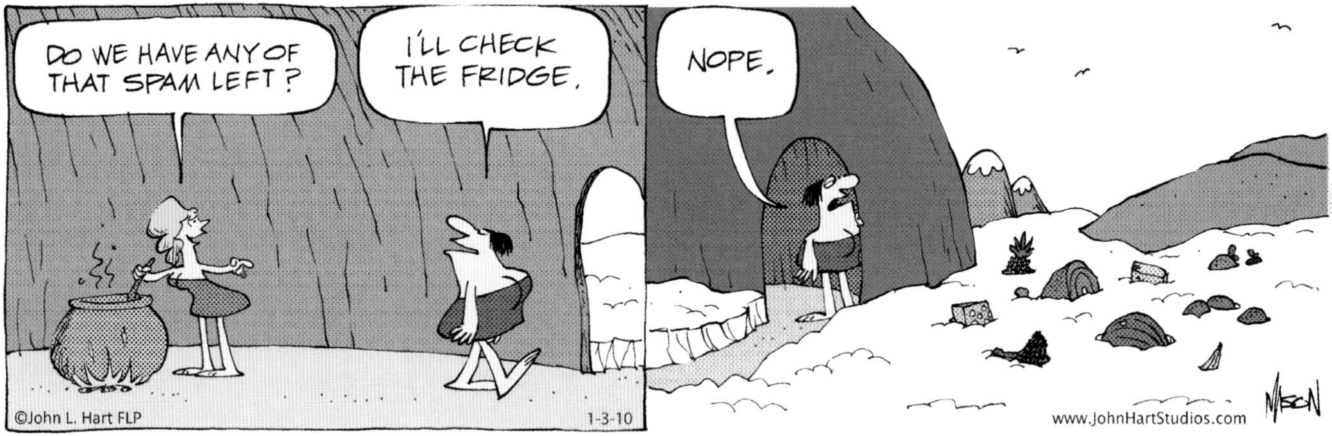
DO WE HAVE ANY OF THAT SPAM LEFT?
I'LL CHECK THE FRIDGE.
NOPE.
©John L. Hart FLP
1-3-10
www.JohnHartStudios.com

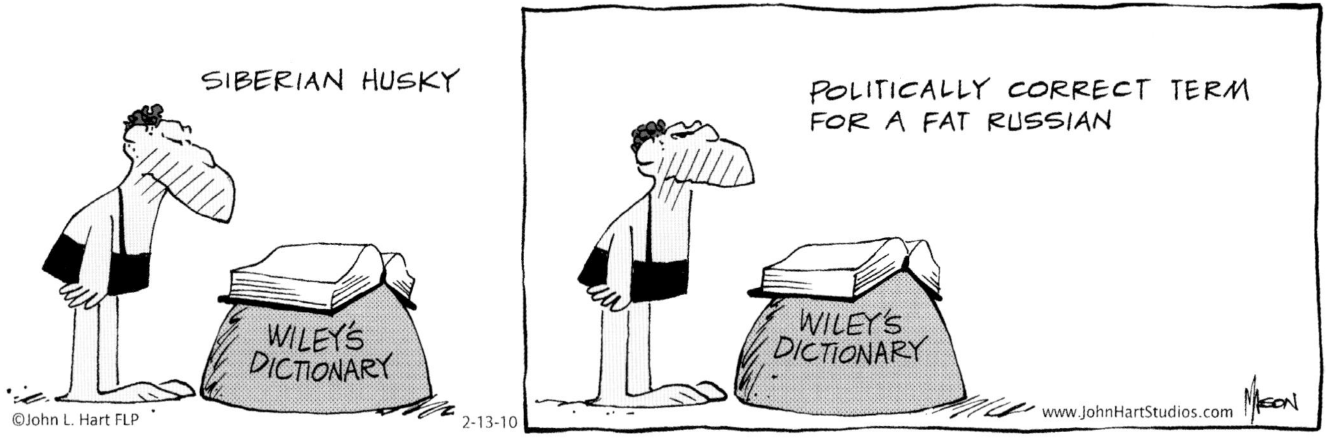
SIBERIAN HUSKY
WILEY'S DICTIONARY
POLITICALLY CORRECT TERM FOR A FAT RUSSIAN
WILEY'S DICTIONARY
©John L. Hart FLP
2-13-10
www.JohnHartStudios.com

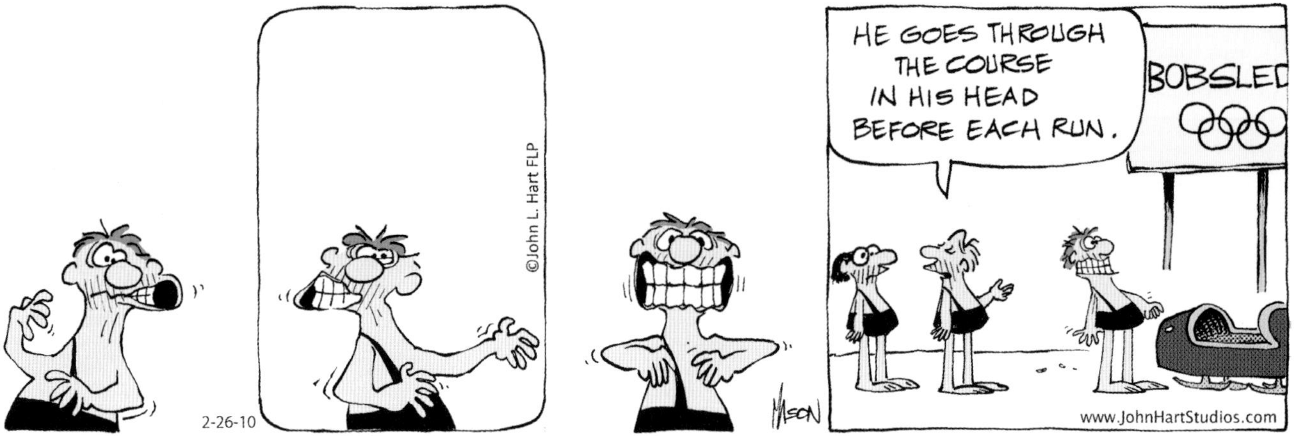
©John L. Hart FLP
2-26-10
HE GOES THROUGH THE COURSE IN HIS HEAD BEFORE EACH RUN.
BOBSLED
www.JohnHartStudios.com

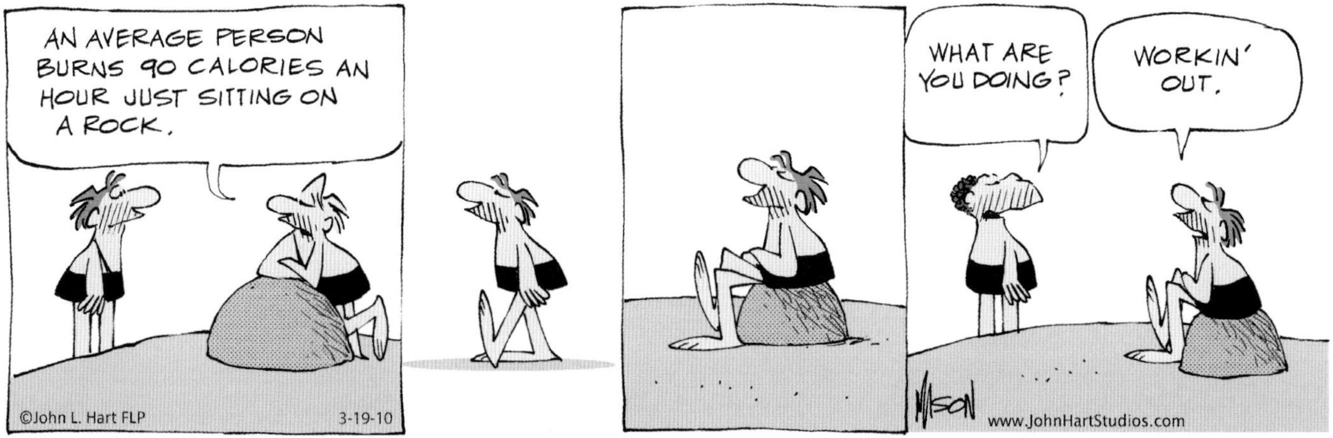
AN AVERAGE PERSON BURNS 90 CALORIES AN HOUR JUST SITTING ON A ROCK.
©John L. Hart FLP
3-19-10
WHAT ARE YOU DOING?
WORKIN' OUT.
www.JohnHartStudios.com

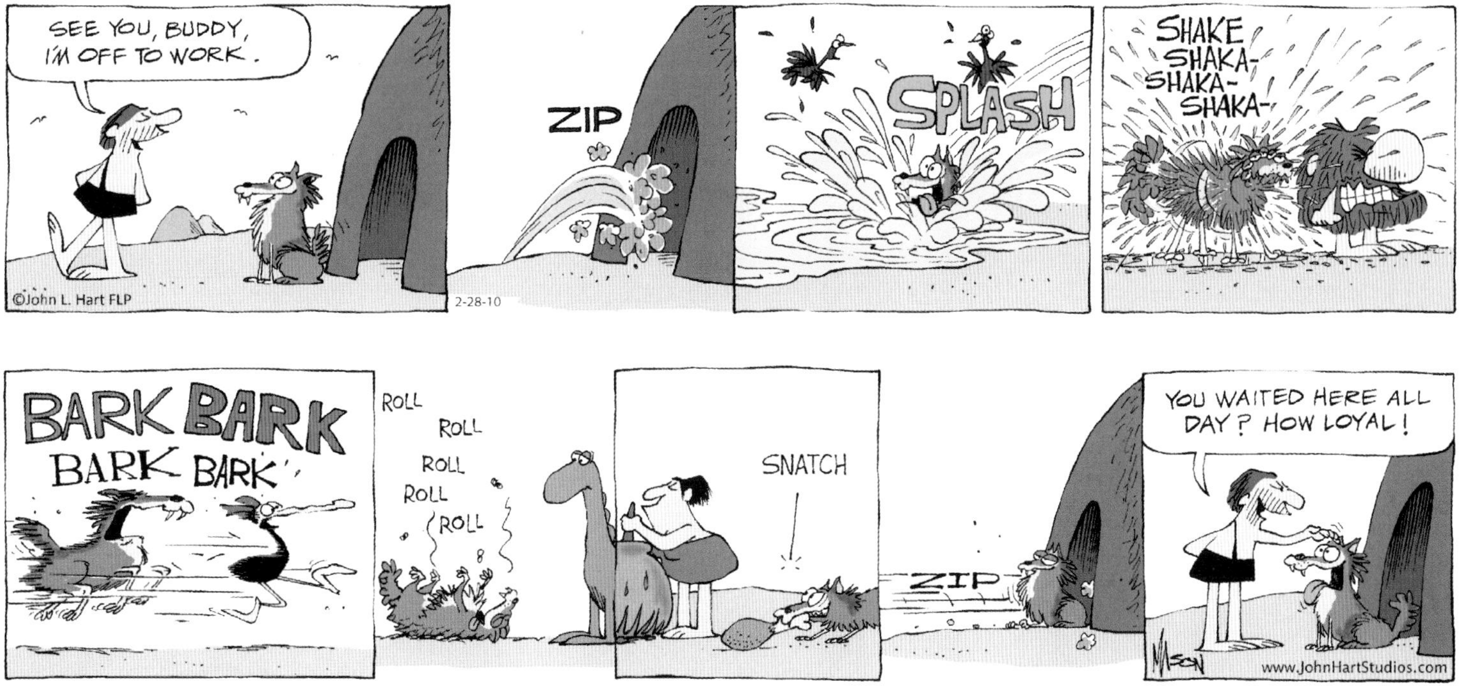
SEE YOU, BUDDY, I'M OFF TO WORK.
©John L. Hart FLP
2-28-10
ZIP
SPLASH
SHAKE SHAKA- SHAKA- SHAKA-
BARK BARK
BARK BARK
ROLL ROLL ROLL ROLL ROLL
SNATCH
ZIP
YOU WAITED HERE ALL DAY? HOW LOYAL!
MASON
www.JohnHartStudios.com

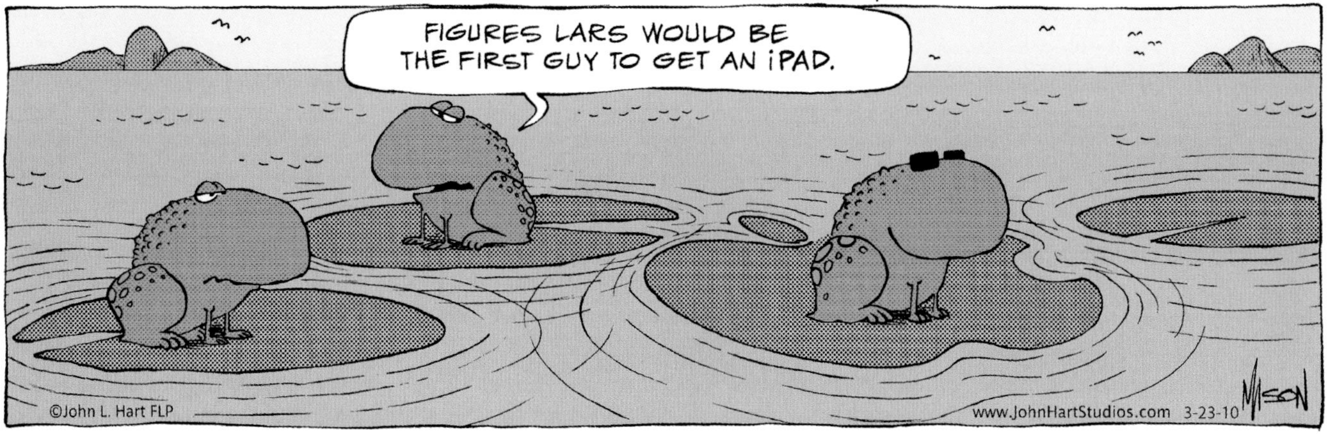
FIGURES LARS WOULD BE THE FIRST GUY TO GET AN iPAD.
©John L. Hart FLP
www.JohnHartStudios.com 3-23-10
MASON

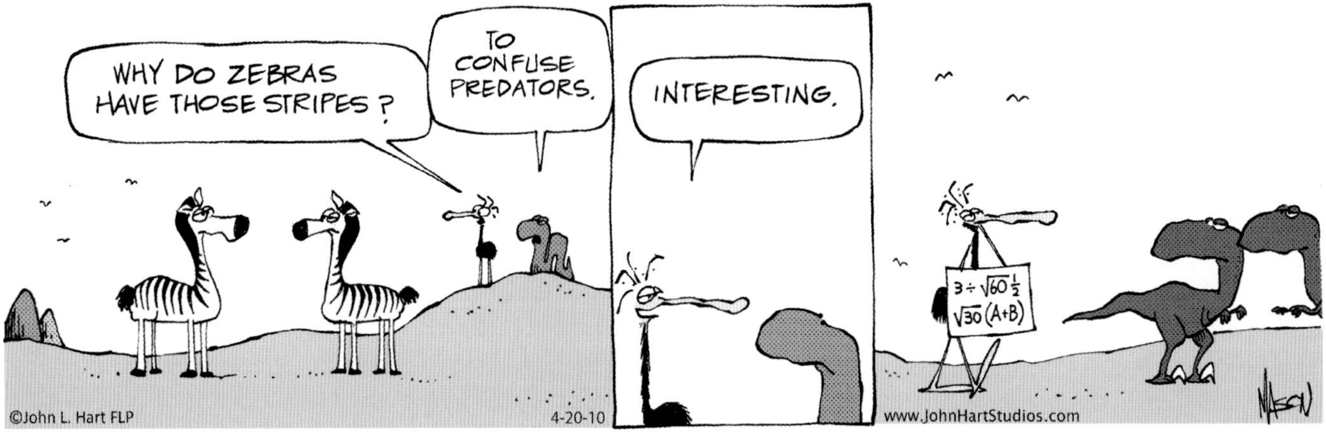
WHY DO ZEBRAS HAVE THOSE STRIPES?
TO CONFUSE PREDATORS.
INTERESTING.
3 ÷ √60 ½
√30 (A+B)
©John L. Hart FLP
4-20-10
www.JohnHartStudios.com
MASON

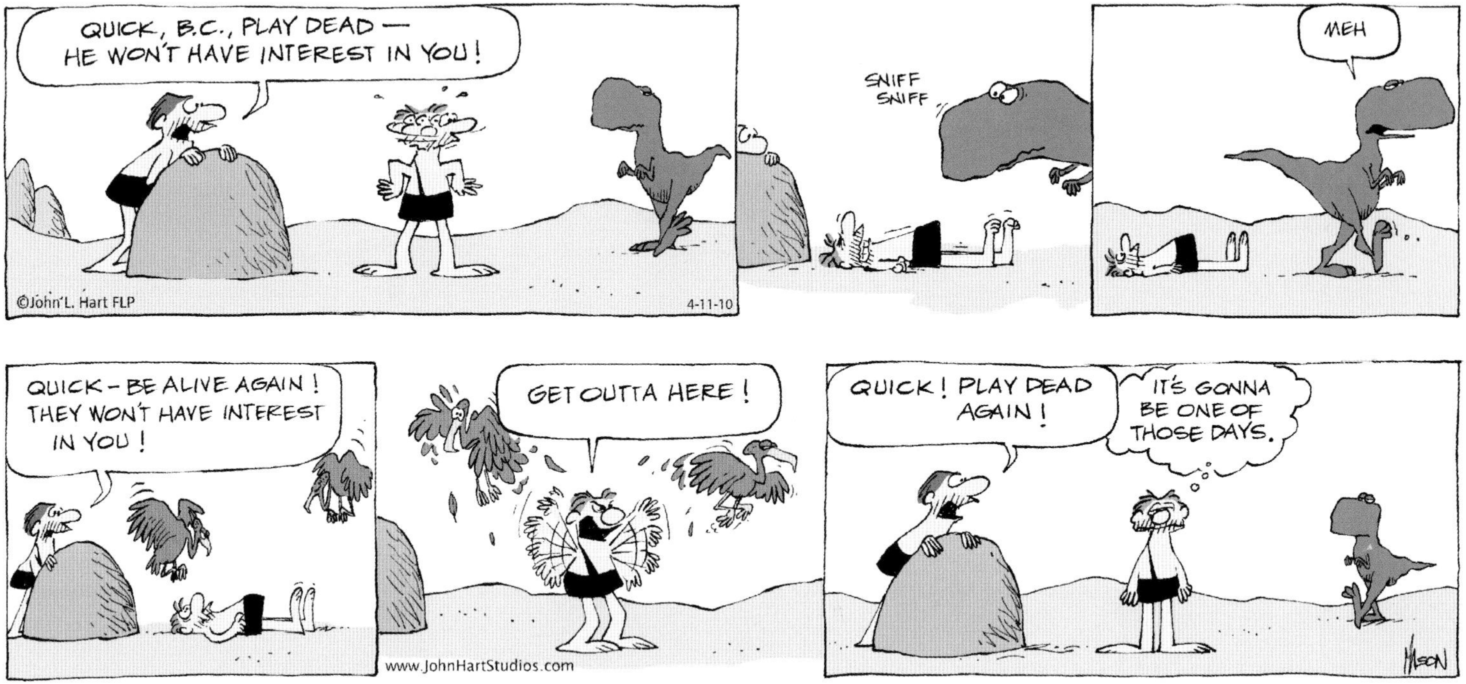
QUICK, B.C., PLAY DEAD — HE WON'T HAVE INTEREST IN YOU!
©John L. Hart FLP
4-11-10
SNIFF SNIFF
MEH
QUICK - BE ALIVE AGAIN! THEY WON'T HAVE INTEREST IN YOU!
GET OUTTA HERE!
www.JohnHartStudios.com
QUICK! PLAY DEAD AGAIN!
IT'S GONNA BE ONE OF THOSE DAYS.
MASON

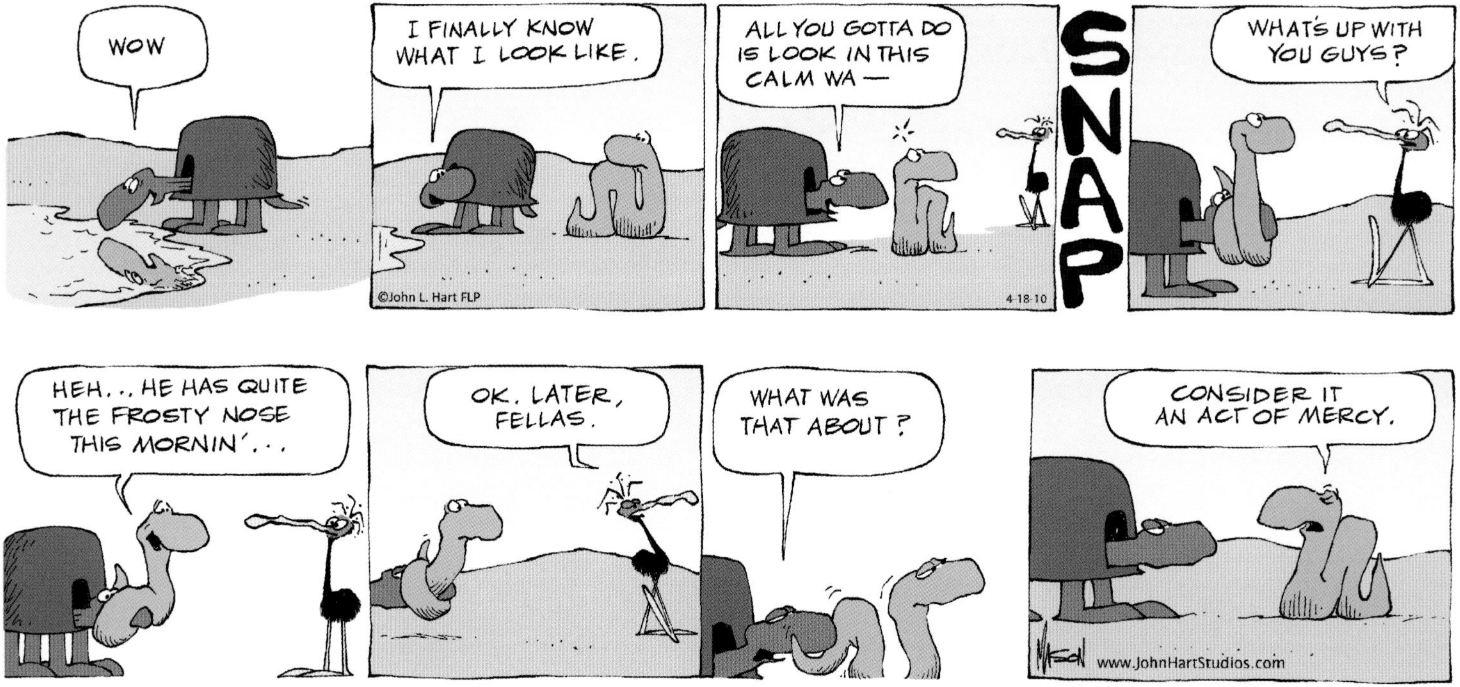
WOW
I FINALLY KNOW WHAT I LOOK LIKE.
©John L. Hart FLP
ALL YOU GOTTA DO IS LOOK IN THIS CALM WA—
4-18-10
SNAP
WHAT'S UP WITH YOU GUYS?
HEH... HE HAS QUITE THE FROSTY NOSE THIS MORNIN'...
OK. LATER, FELLAS.
WHAT WAS THAT ABOUT?
CONSIDER IT AN ACT OF MERCY.
www.JohnHartStudios.com

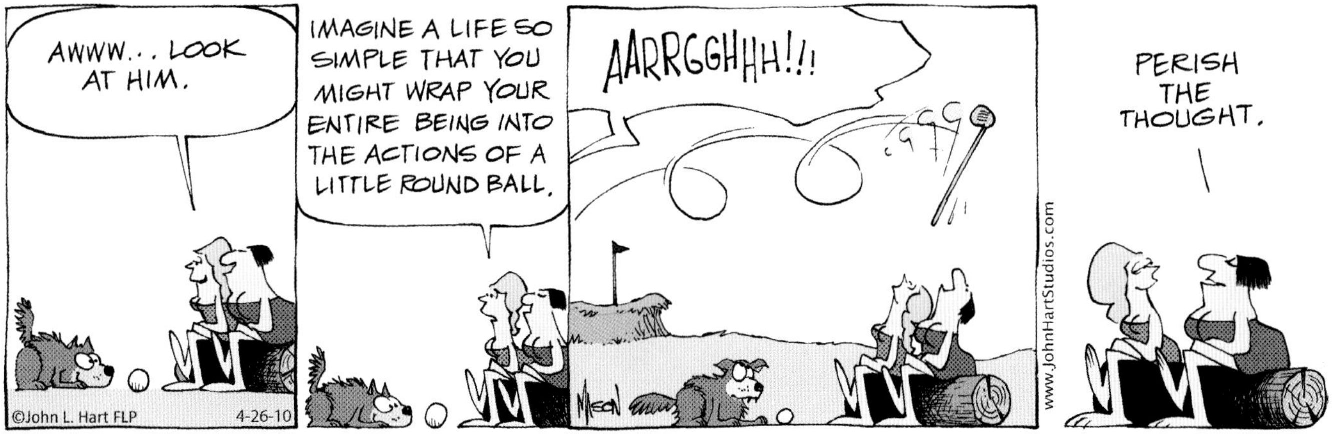
AWWW... LOOK AT HIM.
IMAGINE A LIFE SO SIMPLE THAT YOU MIGHT WRAP YOUR ENTIRE BEING INTO THE ACTIONS OF A LITTLE ROUND BALL.
AARRGGHHHH!!!
PERISH THE THOUGHT.
©John L. Hart FLP
4-26-10
www.JohnHartStudios.com

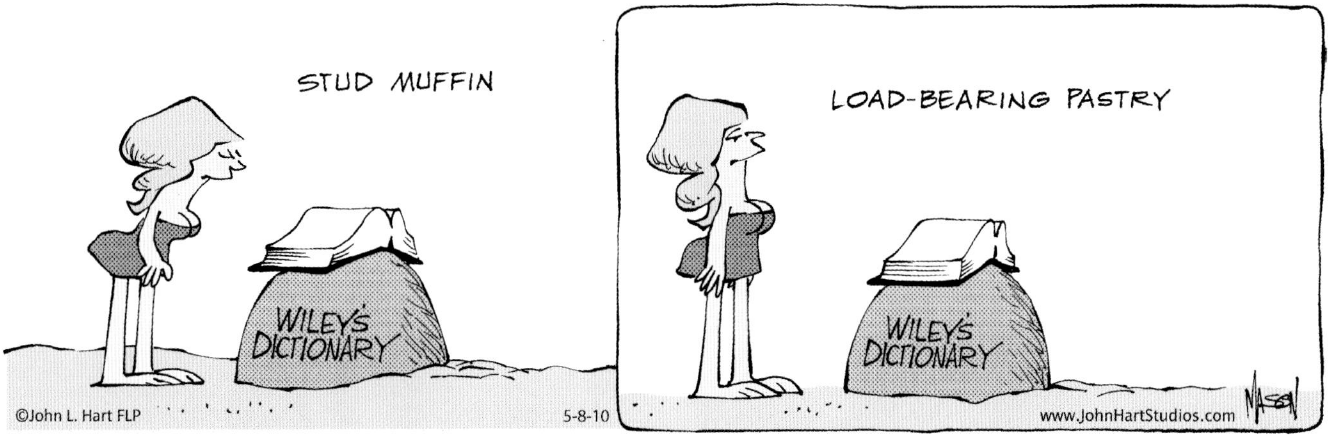
STUD MUFFIN
WILEY'S DICTIONARY
LOAD-BEARING PASTRY
WILEY'S DICTIONARY
©John L. Hart FLP
5-8-10
www.JohnHartStudios.com

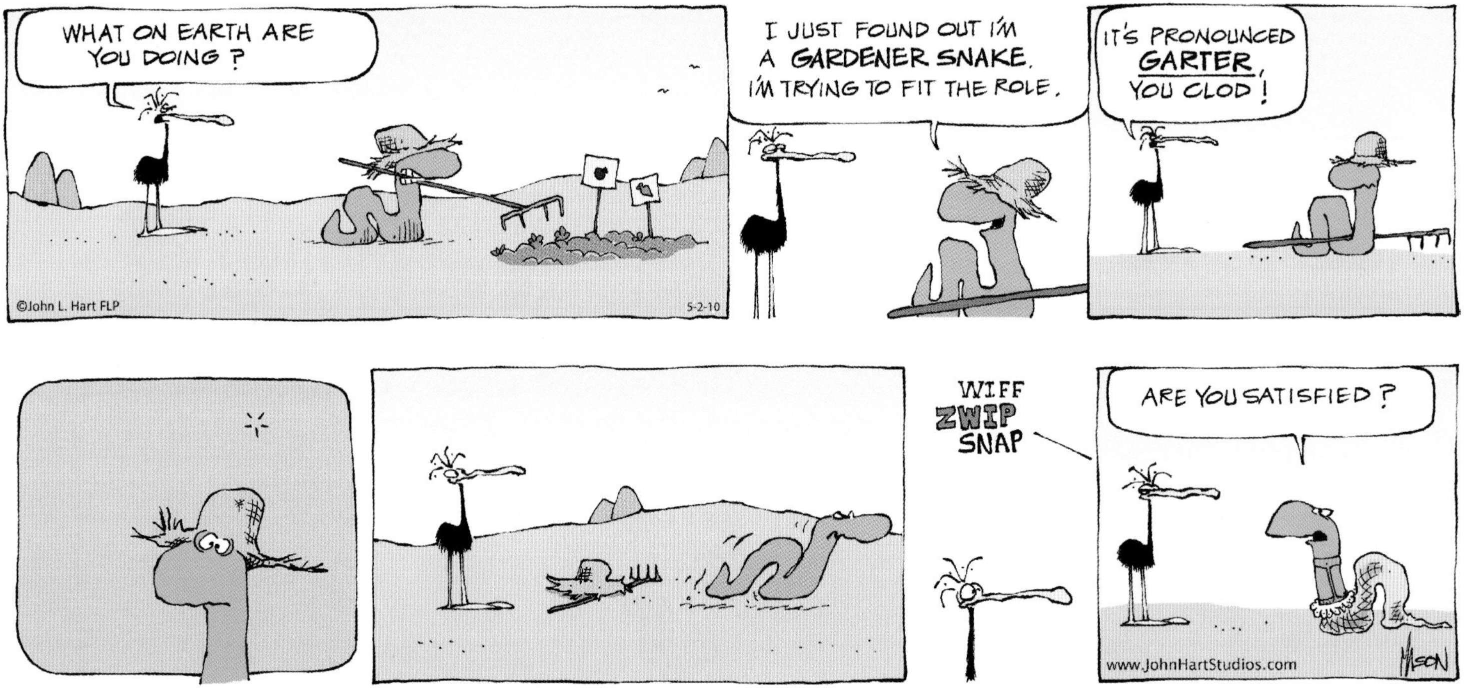
WHAT ON EARTH ARE YOU DOING ?
©John L. Hart FLP
5-2-10
I JUST FOUND OUT I'M A GARDENER SNAKE. I'M TRYING TO FIT THE ROLE.
IT'S PRONOUNCED GARTER, YOU CLOD !
WIFF
ZWIP
SNAP
ARE YOU SATISFIED ?
www.JohnHartStudios.com
MASON

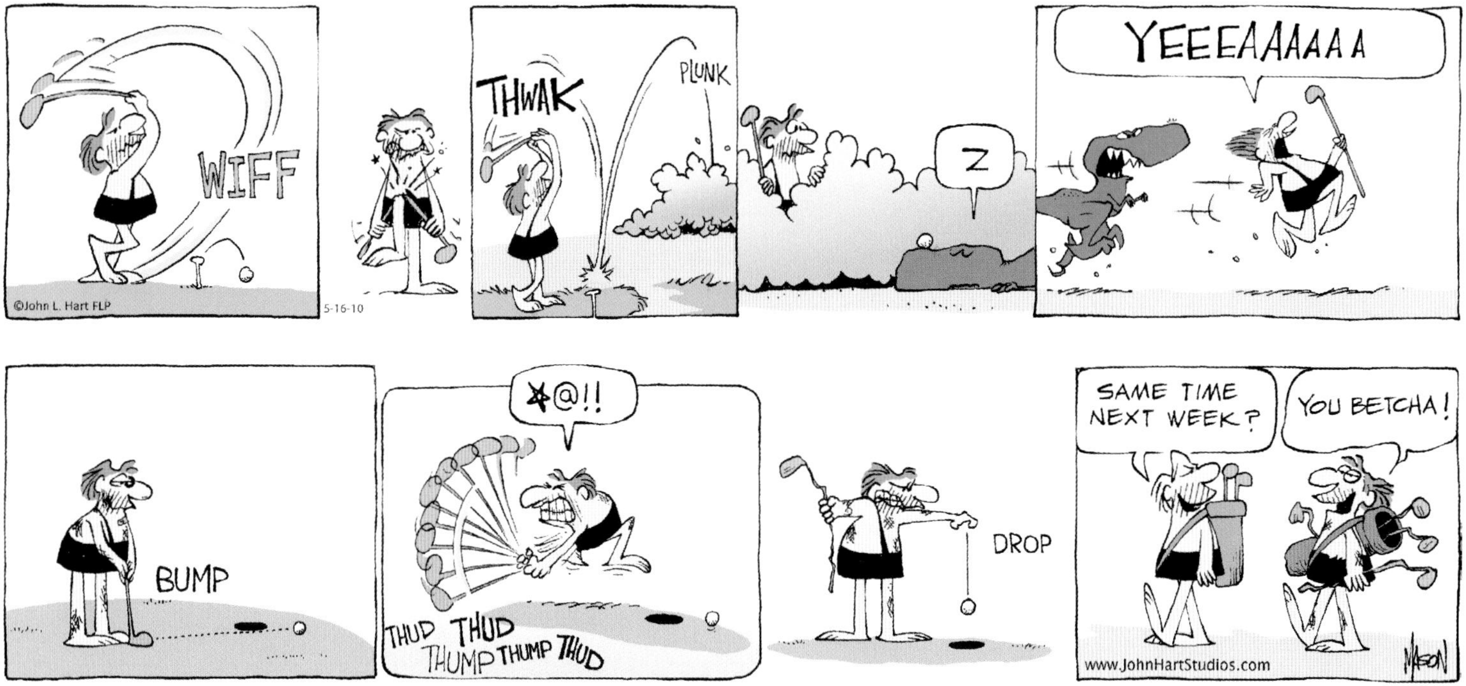
©John L. Hart FLP
WIFF
5-16-10
THWAK
PLUNK
Z
YEEEAAAAAA
BUMP
☆@!!
THUD THUD
THUMP THUMP THUD
DROP
SAME TIME NEXT WEEK?
YOU BETCHA!
www.JohnHartStudios.com
MASON

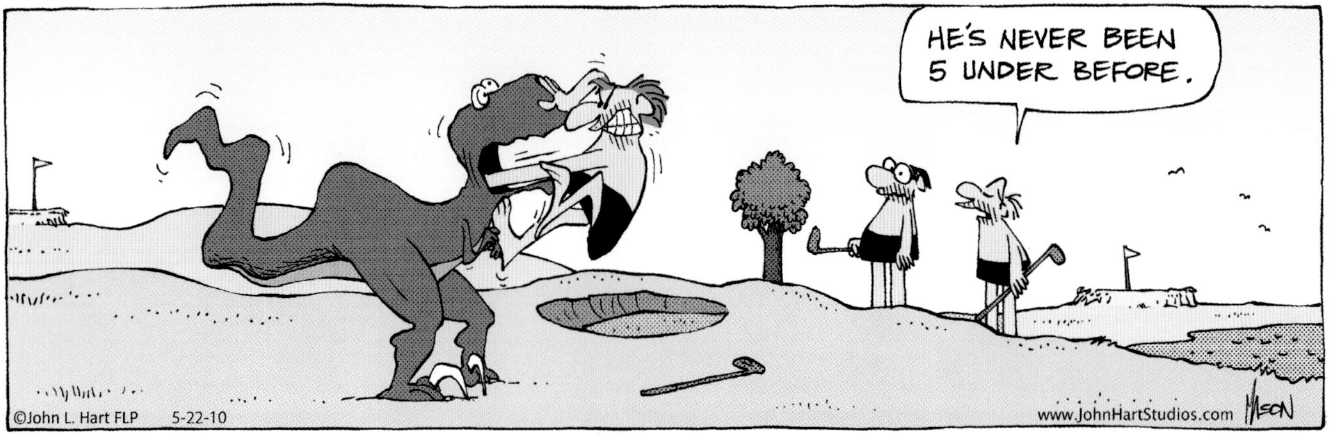
HE'S NEVER BEEN 5 UNDER BEFORE.
©John L. Hart FLP 5-22-10
www.JohnHartStudios.com
MASON

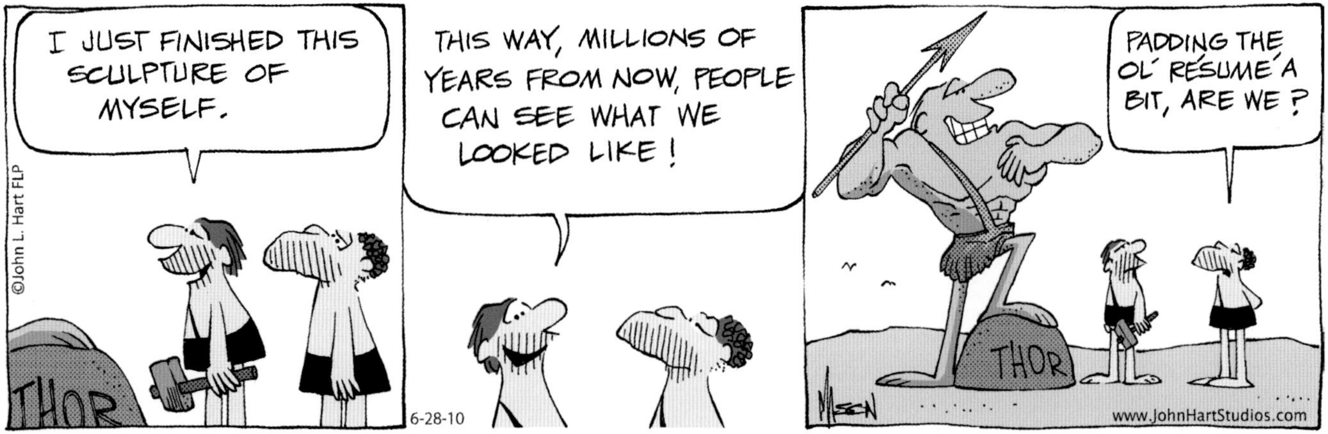
I JUST FINISHED THIS SCULPTURE OF MYSELF.
THIS WAY, MILLIONS OF YEARS FROM NOW, PEOPLE CAN SEE WHAT WE LOOKED LIKE!
PADDING THE OL' RÉSUMÉ A BIT, ARE WE?
THOR
THOR
©John L. Hart FLP
6-28-10
MASON
www.JohnHartStudios.com

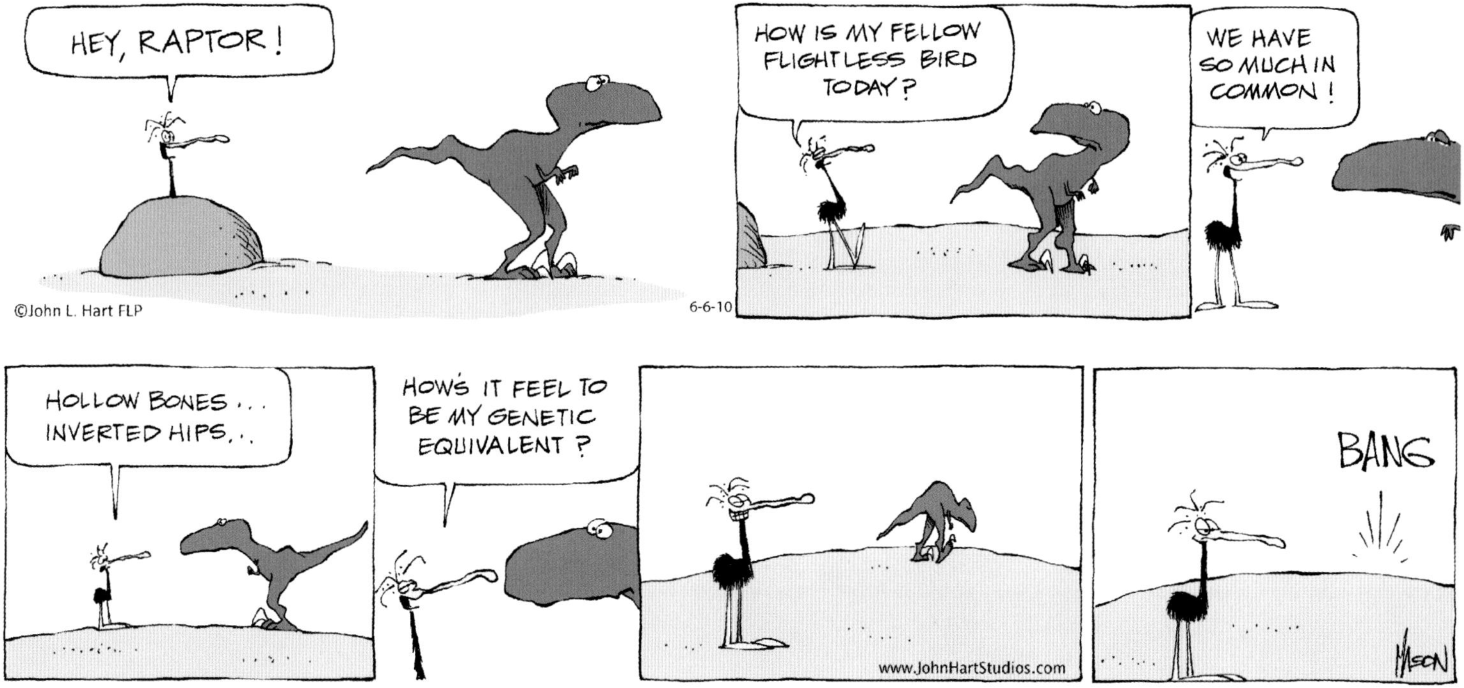

HEY, RAPTOR!
©John L. Hart FLP
6-6-10
HOW IS MY FELLOW FLIGHTLESS BIRD TODAY?
WE HAVE SO MUCH IN COMMON!
HOLLOW BONES... INVERTED HIPS...
HOW'S IT FEEL TO BE MY GENETIC EQUIVALENT?
www.JohnHartStudios.com
BANG
MASON

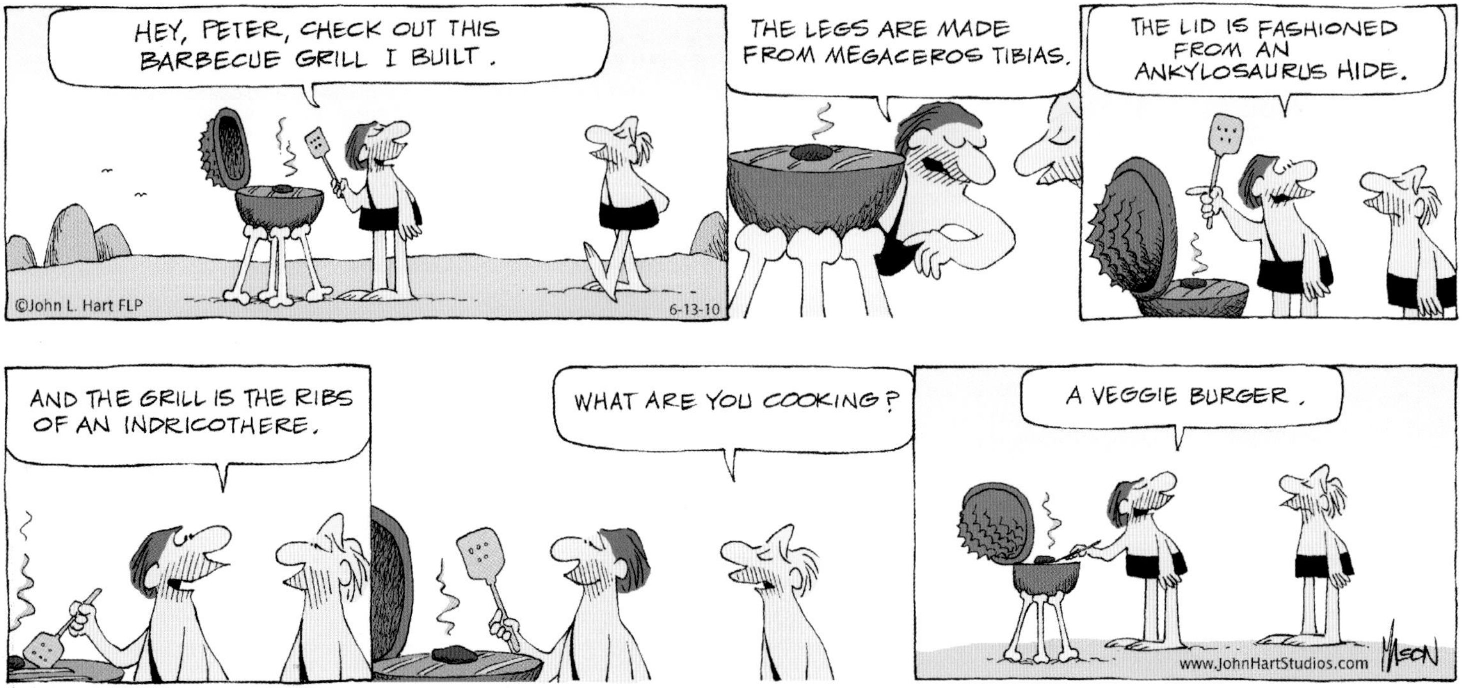
HEY, PETER, CHECK OUT THIS BARBECUE GRILL I BUILT.
THE LEGS ARE MADE FROM MEGACEROS TIBIAS.
THE LID IS FASHIONED FROM AN ANKYLOSAURUS HIDE.
AND THE GRILL IS THE RIBS OF AN INDRICOTHERE.
WHAT ARE YOU COOKING?
A VEGGIE BURGER.
©John L. Hart FLP
6-13-10
www.JohnHartStudios.com
MASON

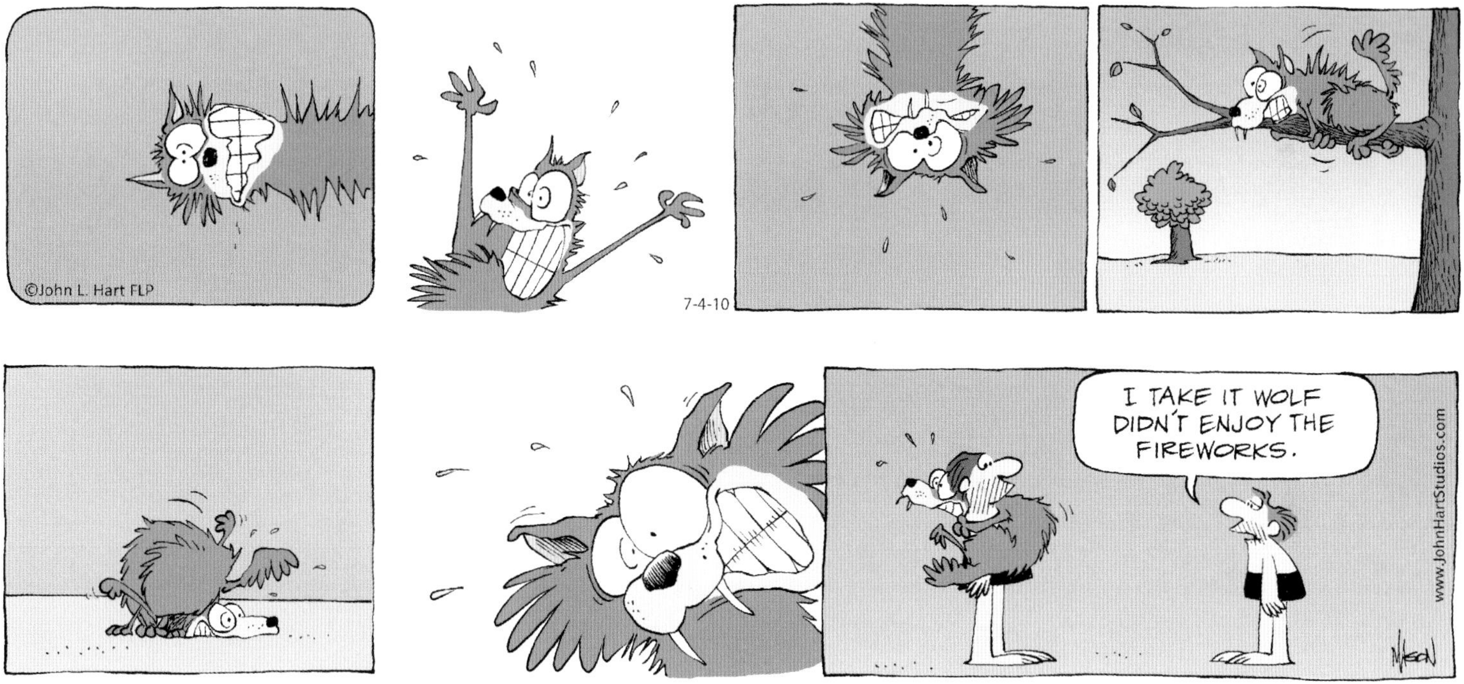
©John L. Hart FLP
7-4-10
I TAKE IT WOLF DIDN'T ENJOY THE FIREWORKS.
www.JohnHartStudios.com

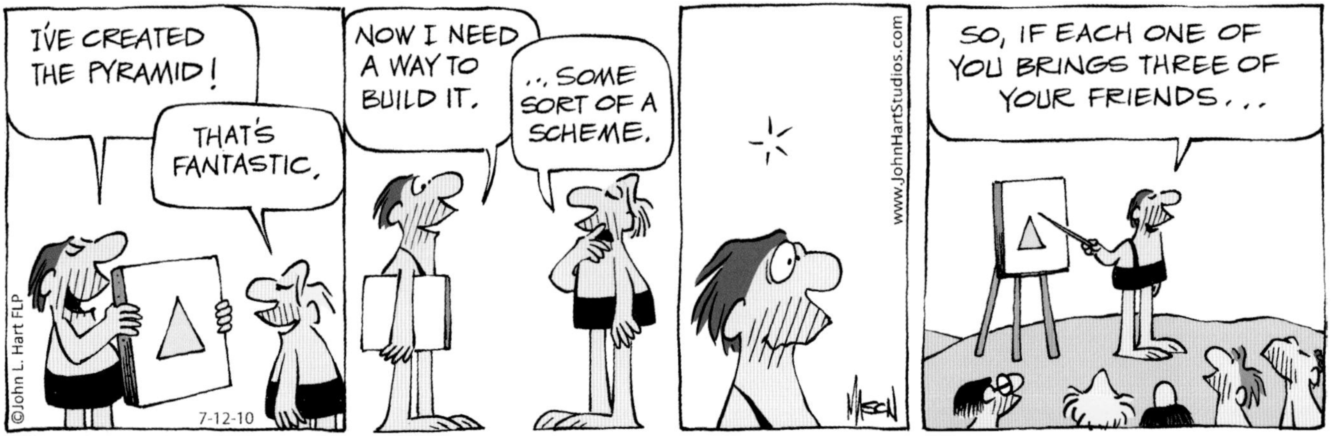
I'VE CREATED THE PYRAMID!
THAT'S FANTASTIC.
NOW I NEED A WAY TO BUILD IT.
... SOME SORT OF A SCHEME.
SO, IF EACH ONE OF YOU BRINGS THREE OF YOUR FRIENDS...
©John L. Hart FLP
7-12-10
www.JohnHartStudios.com

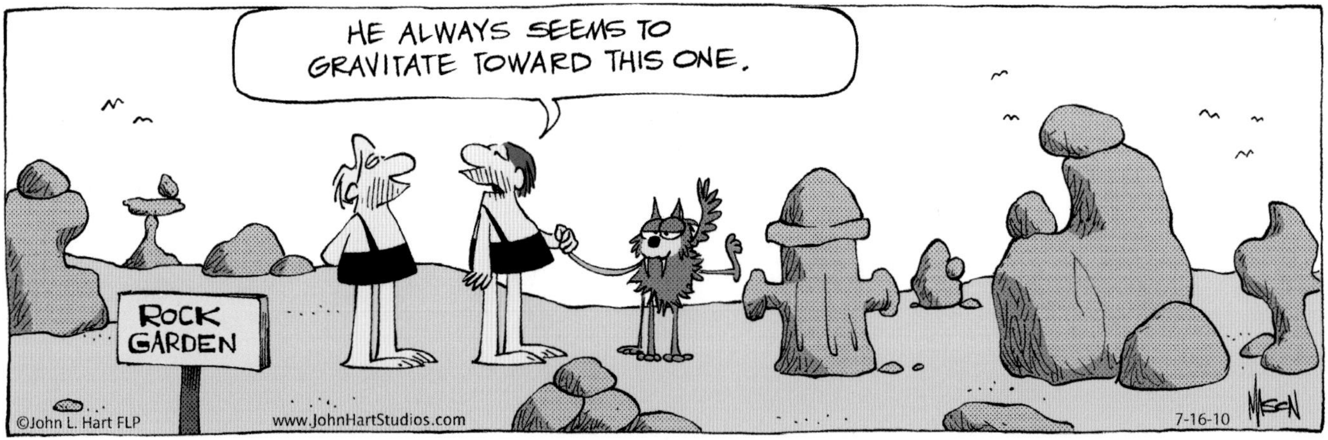
HE ALWAYS SEEMS TO GRAVITATE TOWARD THIS ONE.
ROCK GARDEN
©John L. Hart FLP
www.JohnHartStudios.com
7-16-10

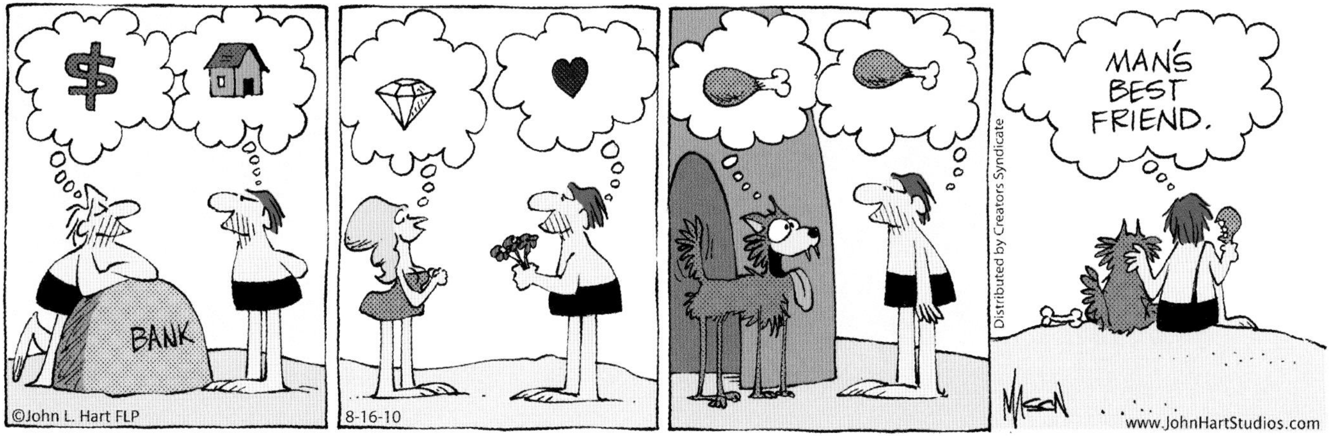
BANK
MAN'S BEST FRIEND.
©John L. Hart FLP
8-16-10
Distributed by Creators Syndicate
MASON
www.JohnHartStudios.com

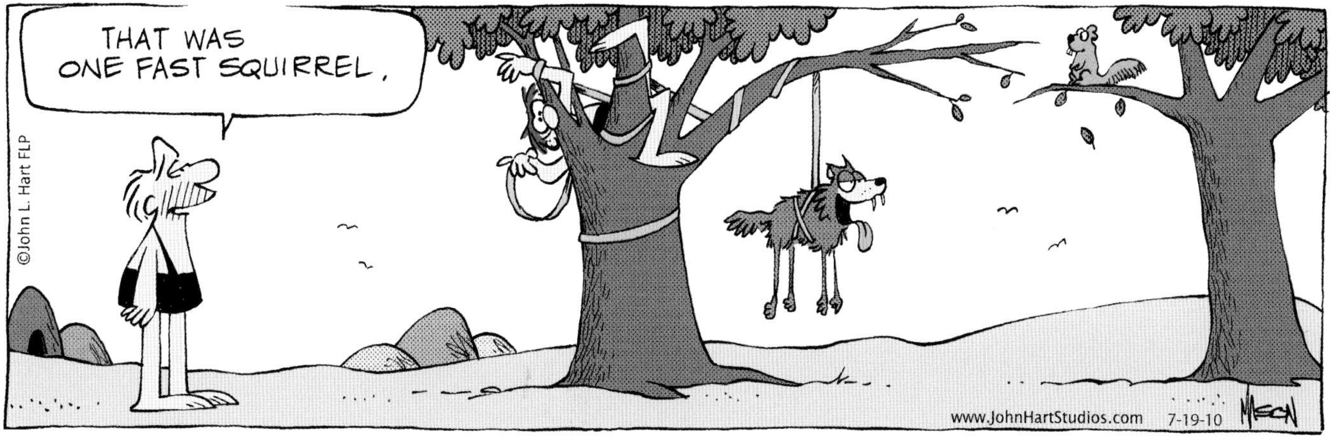
THAT WAS ONE FAST SQUIRREL.
©John L. Hart FLP
www.JohnHartStudios.com
7-19-10
MASON

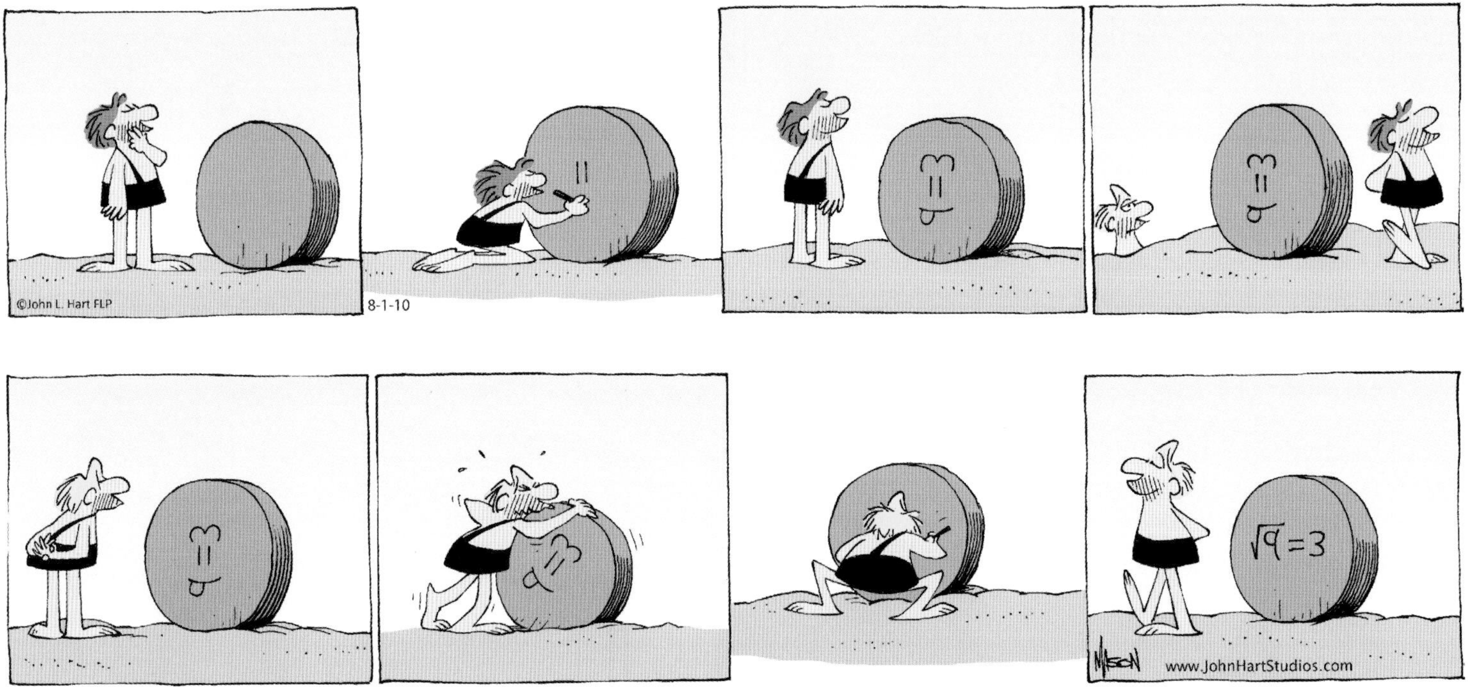
©John L. Hart FLP
8-1-10
√9 =3
www.JohnHartStudios.com

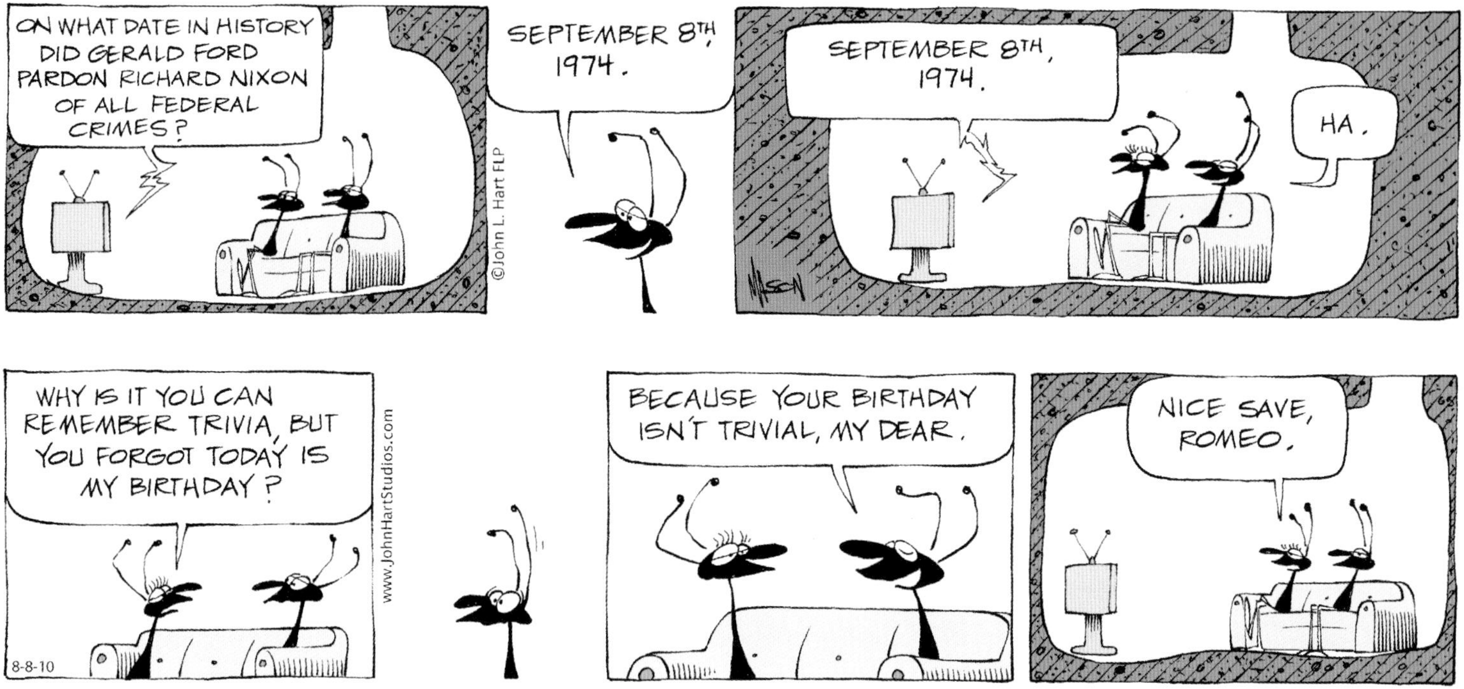
ON WHAT DATE IN HISTORY DID GERALD FORD PARDON RICHARD NIXON OF ALL FEDERAL CRIMES?
SEPTEMBER 8TH, 1974.
SEPTEMBER 8TH, 1974.
HA.
WHY IS IT YOU CAN REMEMBER TRIVIA, BUT YOU FORGOT TODAY IS MY BIRTHDAY?
BECAUSE YOUR BIRTHDAY ISN'T TRIVIAL, MY DEAR.
NICE SAVE, ROMEO.
©John L. Hart FLP
www.JohnHartStudios.com
8-8-10

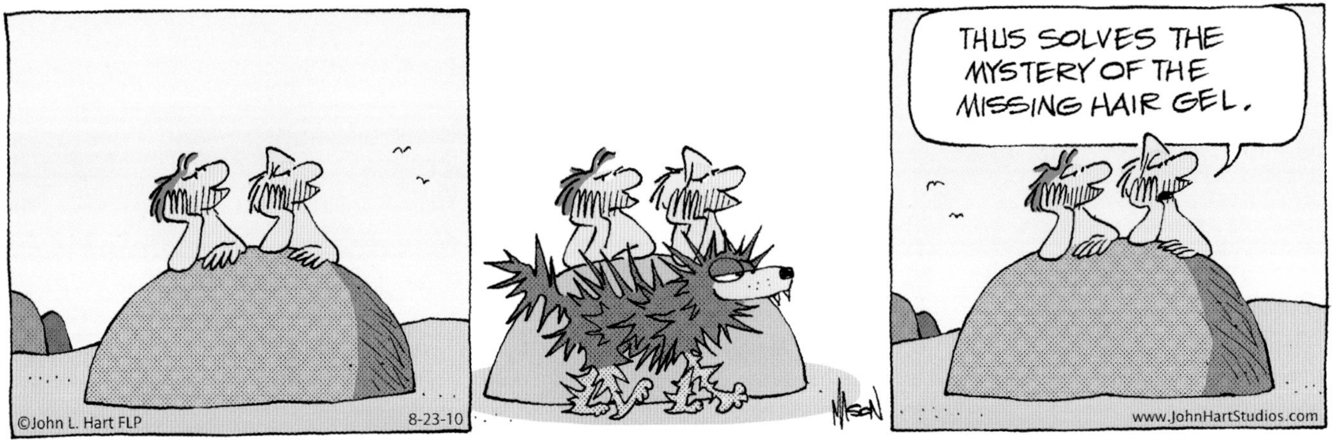
©John L. Hart FLP
8-23-10
THUS SOLVES THE MYSTERY OF THE MISSING HAIR GEL.
www.JohnHartStudios.com

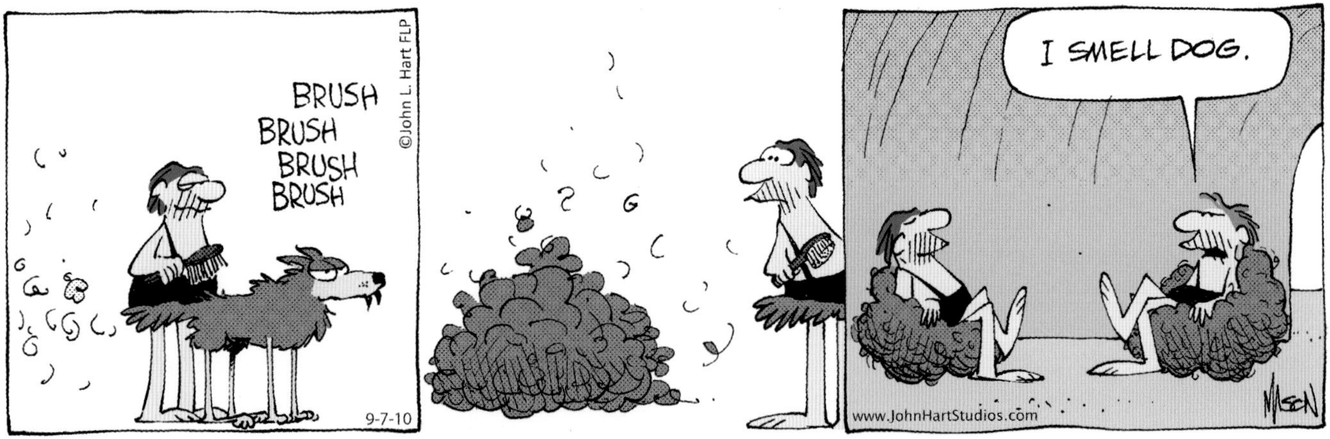
©John L. Hart FLP
BRUSH
BRUSH
BRUSH
BRUSH
9-7-10
I SMELL DOG.
www.JohnHartStudios.com

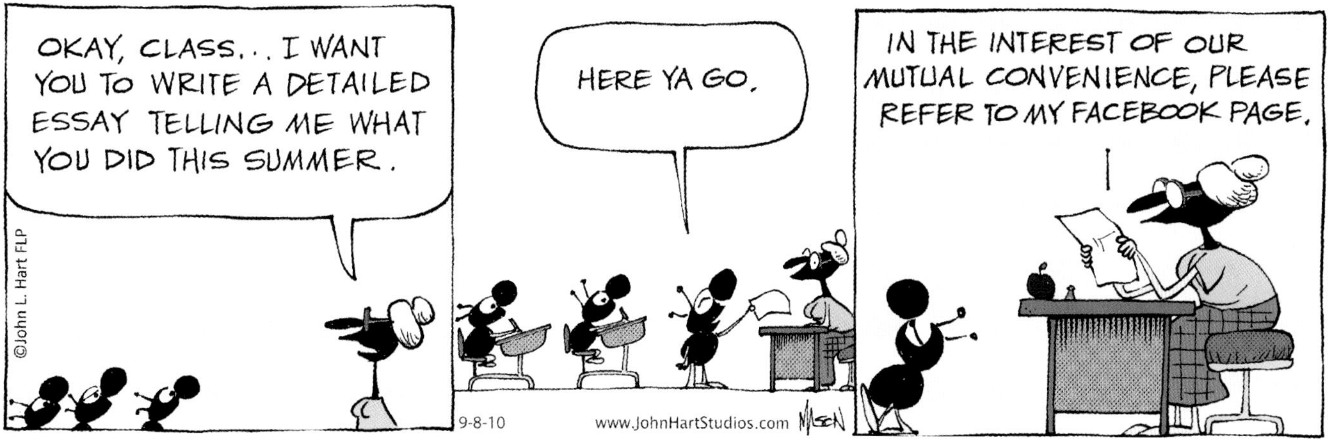
OKAY, CLASS... I WANT YOU TO WRITE A DETAILED ESSAY TELLING ME WHAT YOU DID THIS SUMMER.
HERE YA GO.
IN THE INTEREST OF OUR MUTUAL CONVENIENCE, PLEASE REFER TO MY FACEBOOK PAGE.
©John L. Hart FLP
9-8-10
www.JohnHartStudios.com
MASON

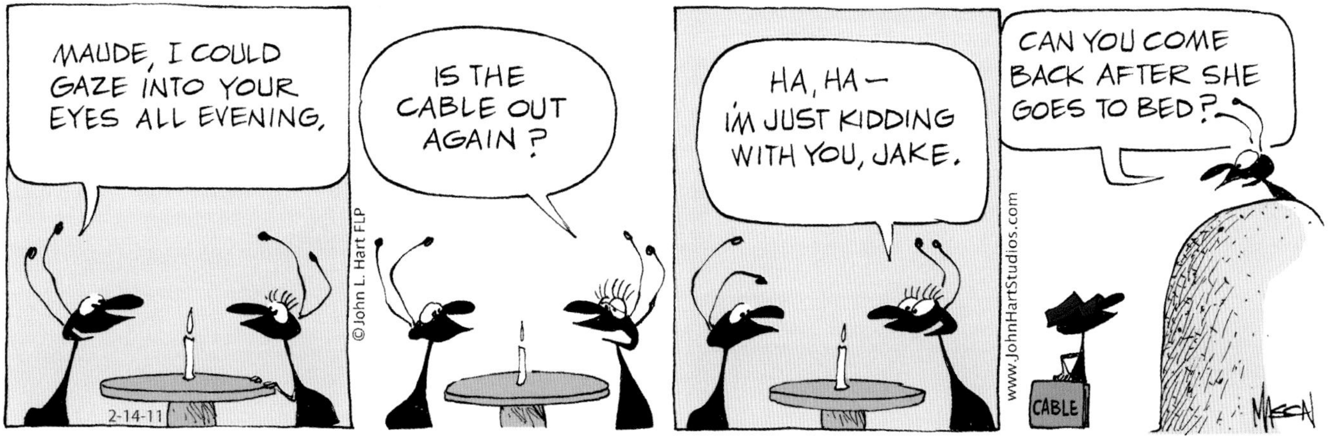
MAUDE, I COULD GAZE INTO YOUR EYES ALL EVENING.
IS THE CABLE OUT AGAIN?
HA, HA — I'M JUST KIDDING WITH YOU, JAKE.
CAN YOU COME BACK AFTER SHE GOES TO BED?
CABLE
©John L. Hart FLP
2-14-11
www.JohnHartStudios.com
MASON

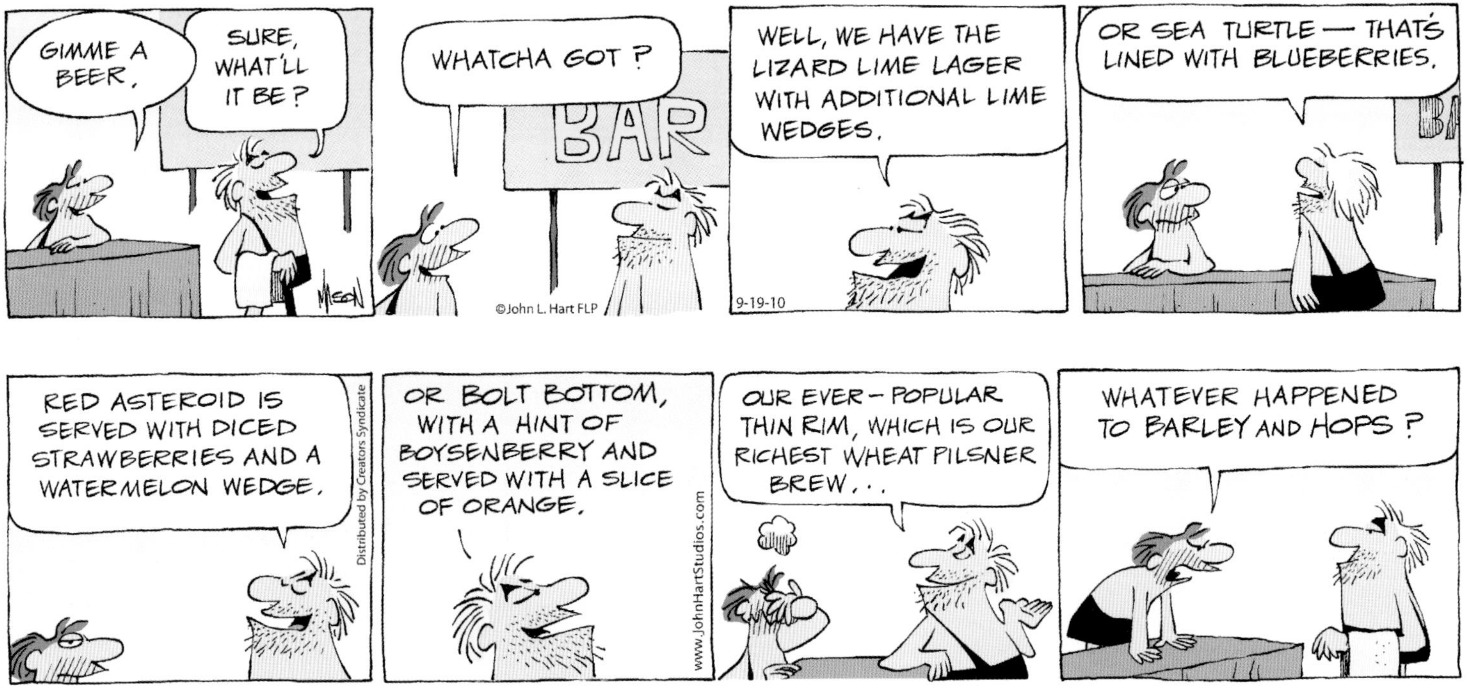

GIMME A BEER.
SURE, WHAT'LL IT BE?
WHATCHA GOT?
BAR
©John L. Hart FLP
WELL, WE HAVE THE LIZARD LIME LAGER WITH ADDITIONAL LIME WEDGES.
9-19-10
OR SEA TURTLE — THAT'S LINED WITH BLUEBERRIES.
RED ASTEROID IS SERVED WITH DICED STRAWBERRIES AND A WATERMELON WEDGE.
Distributed by Creators Syndicate
OR BOLT BOTTOM, WITH A HINT OF BOYSENBERRY AND SERVED WITH A SLICE OF ORANGE.
www.JohnHartStudios.com
OUR EVER-POPULAR THIN RIM, WHICH IS OUR RICHEST WHEAT PILSNER BREW...
WHATEVER HAPPENED TO BARLEY AND HOPS?

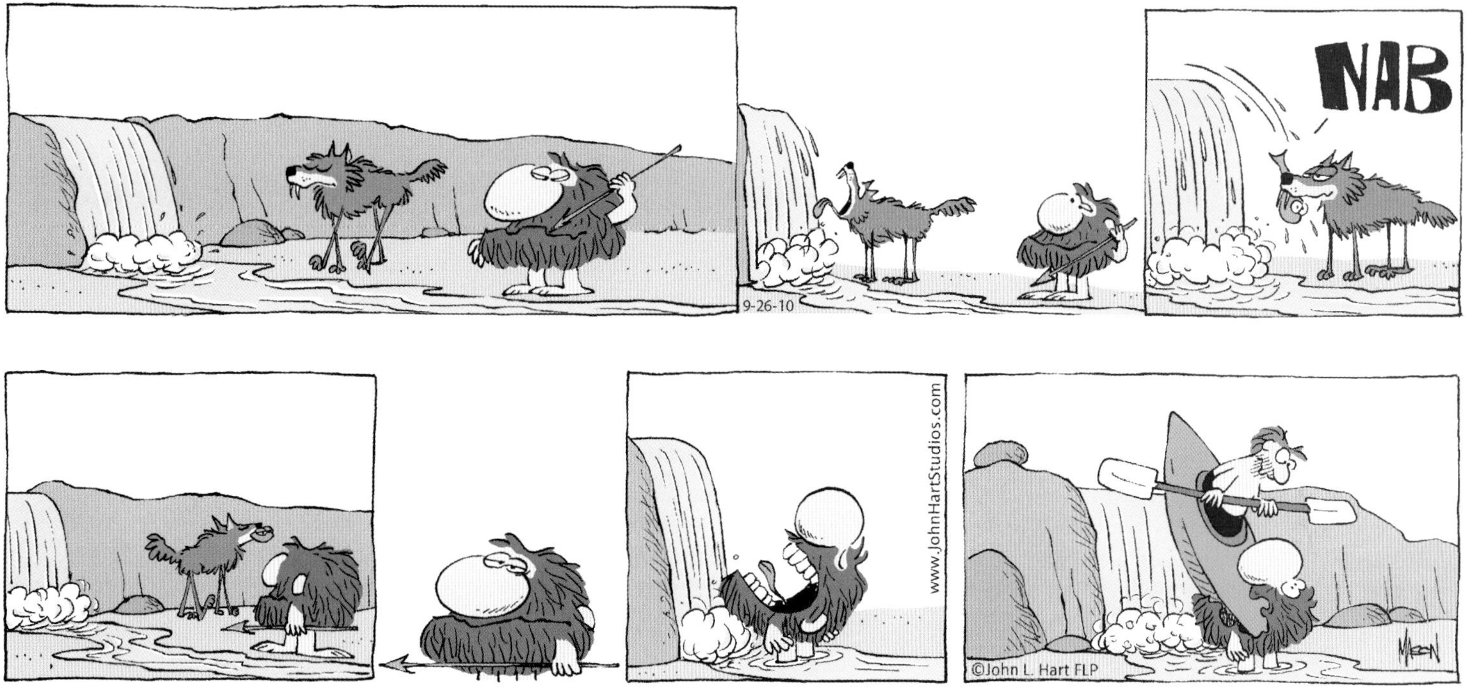
9-26-10
NAB
www.JohnHartStudios.com
©John L. Hart FLP

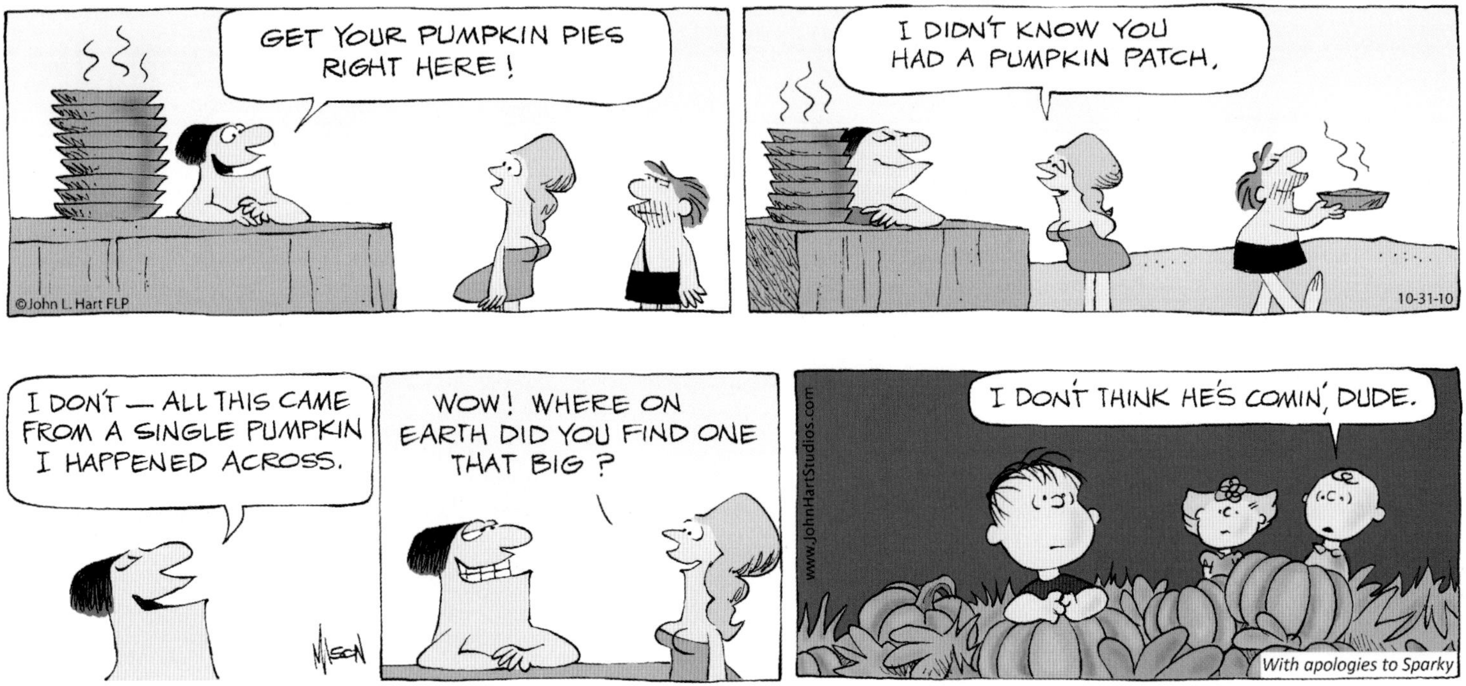
GET YOUR PUMPKIN PIES RIGHT HERE!
©John L. Hart FLP
I DIDN'T KNOW YOU HAD A PUMPKIN PATCH.
10-31-10
I DON'T — ALL THIS CAME FROM A SINGLE PUMPKIN I HAPPENED ACROSS.
WOW! WHERE ON EARTH DID YOU FIND ONE THAT BIG?
www.JohnHartStudios.com
I DON'T THINK HE'S COMIN', DUDE.
With apologies to Sparky

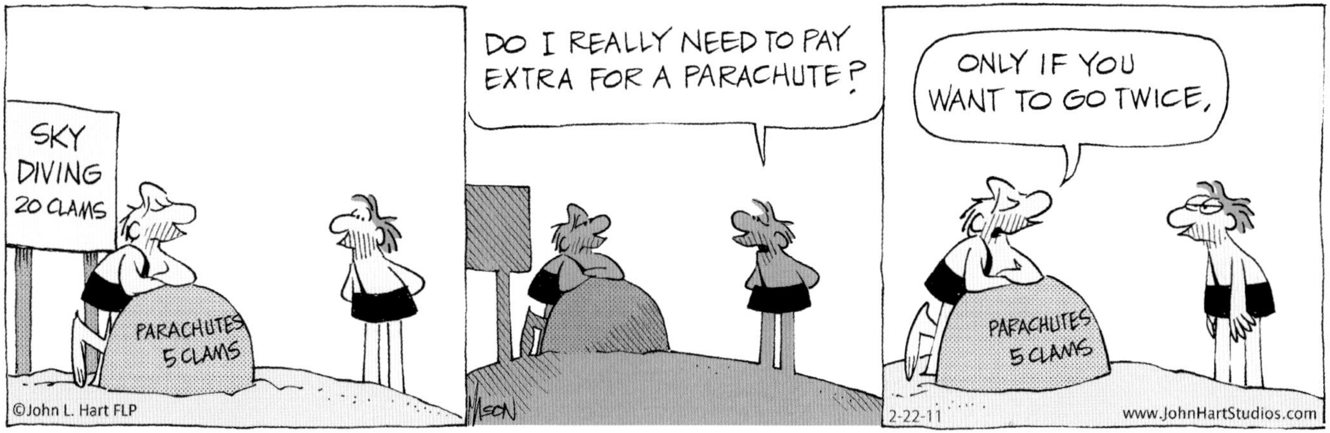
SKY
DIVING
20 CLAMS
PARACHUTES
5 CLAMS
©John L. Hart FLP
DO I REALLY NEED TO PAY EXTRA FOR A PARACHUTE?
MASON
ONLY IF YOU WANT TO GO TWICE,
PARACHUTES
5 CLAMS
2-22-11
www.JohnHartStudios.com

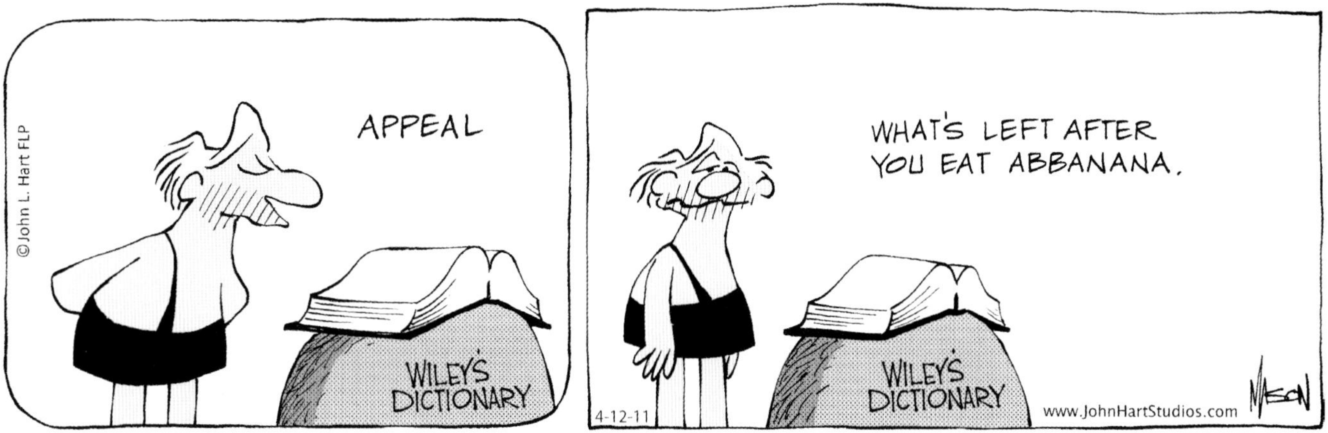
©John L. Hart FLP
APPEAL
WILEY'S
DICTIONARY
WHAT'S LEFT AFTER YOU EAT ABBANANA.
WILEY'S
DICTIONARY
4-12-11
www.JohnHartStudios.com
MASON

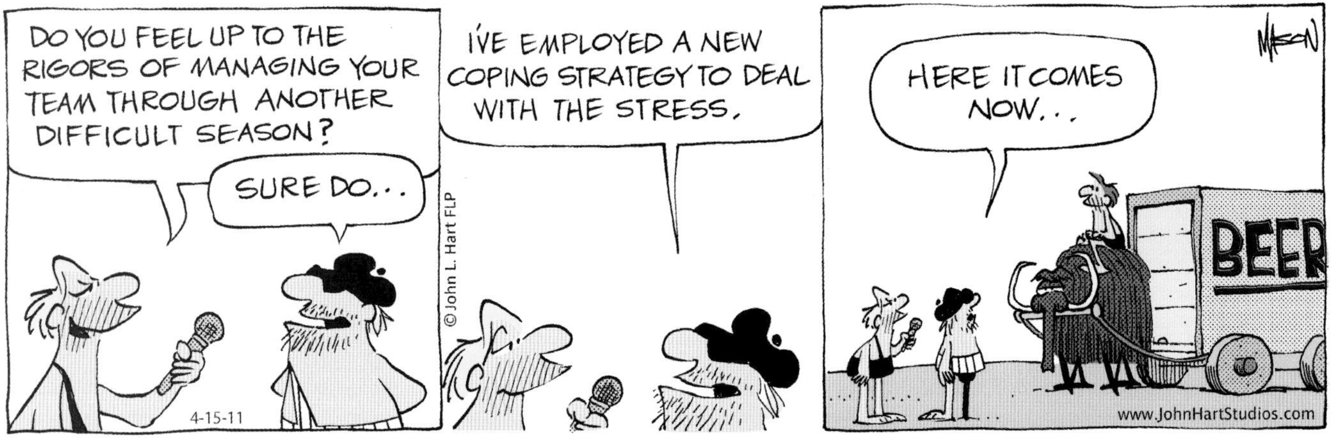
DO YOU FEEL UP TO THE RIGORS OF MANAGING YOUR TEAM THROUGH ANOTHER DIFFICULT SEASON?
SURE DO...
4-15-11
© John L. Hart FLP
I'VE EMPLOYED A NEW COPING STRATEGY TO DEAL WITH THE STRESS.
HERE IT COMES NOW...
MASON
BEER
www.JohnHartStudios.com

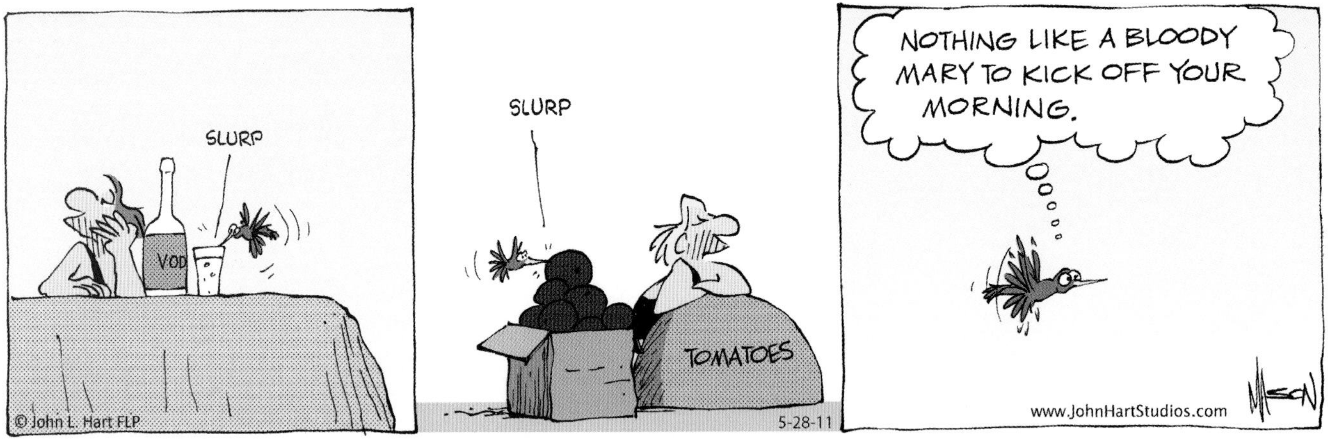
SLURP
VOD
© John L. Hart FLP
SLURP
TOMATOES
5-28-11
NOTHING LIKE A BLOODY MARY TO KICK OFF YOUR MORNING.
www.JohnHartStudios.com
MASON

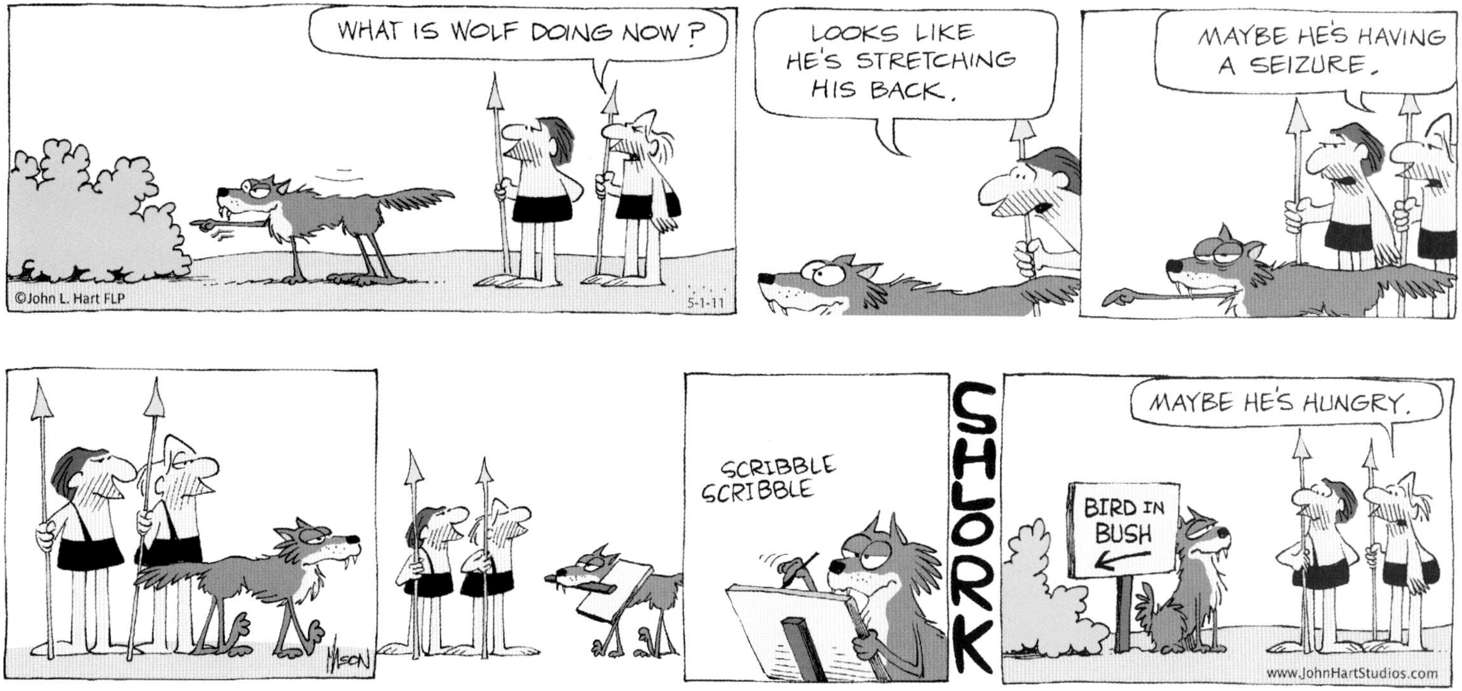
WHAT IS WOLF DOING NOW?
©John L. Hart FLP
5-1-11
LOOKS LIKE HE'S STRETCHING HIS BACK.
MAYBE HE'S HAVING A SEIZURE.
MASON
SCRIBBLE SCRIBBLE
SHLORK
MAYBE HE'S HUNGRY.
BIRD IN BUSH
www.JohnHartStudios.com

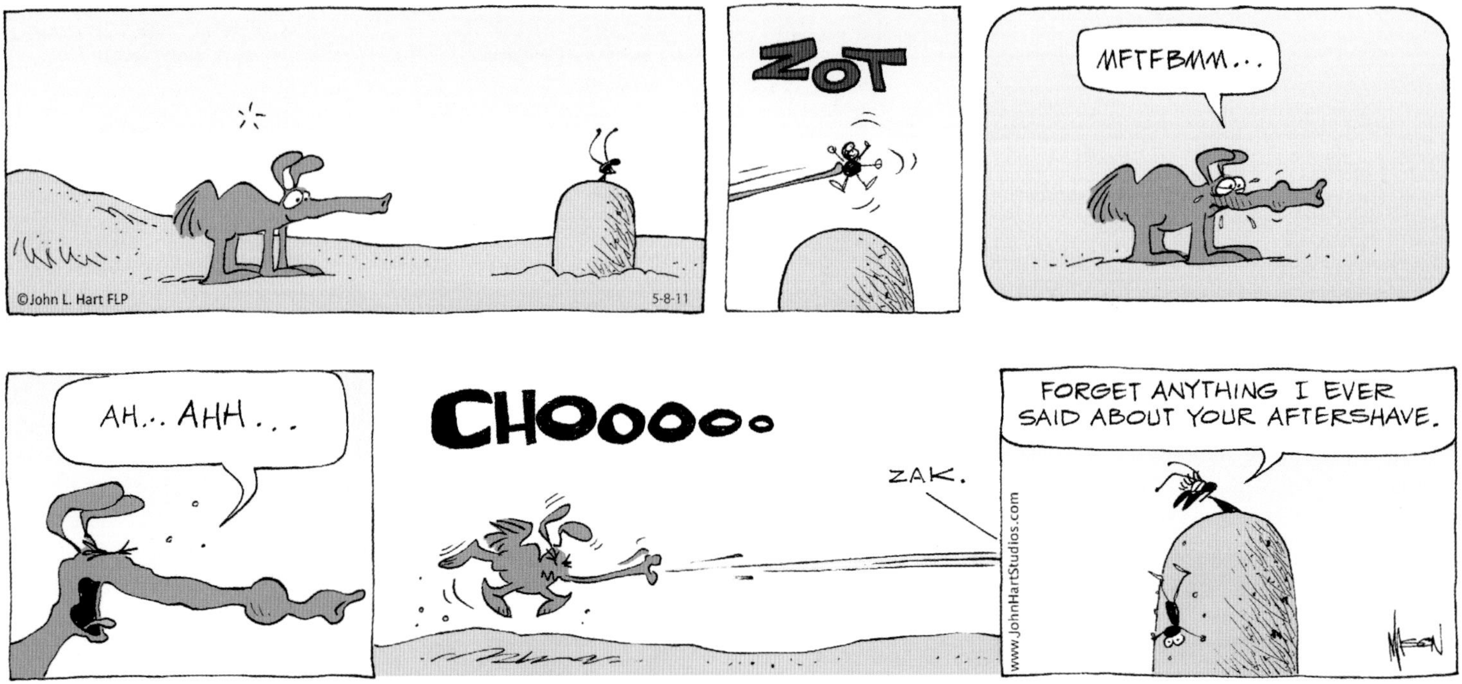
©John L. Hart FLP
5-8-11
ZOT
MFTFBMM...
AH... AHH...
CHOOOOO
ZAK.
www.JohnHartStudios.com
FORGET ANYTHING I EVER SAID ABOUT YOUR AFTERSHAVE.

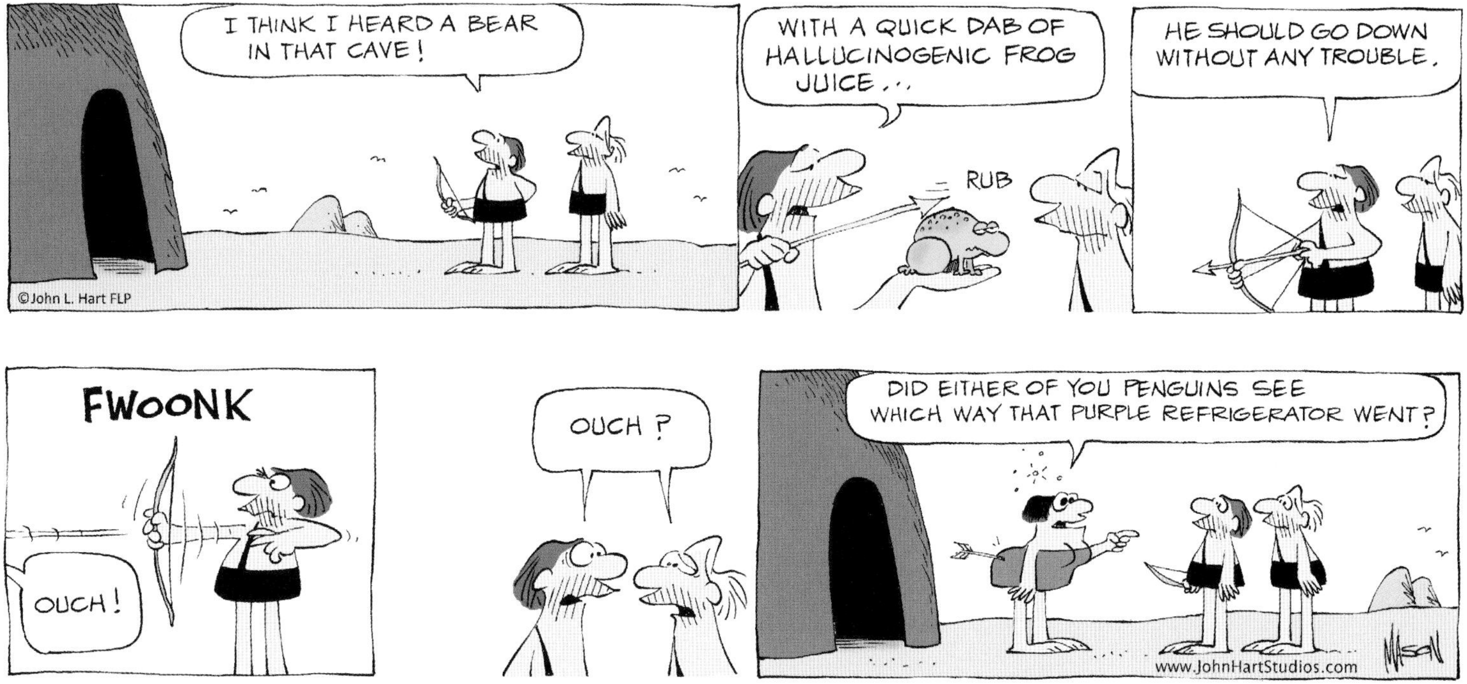
I THINK I HEARD A BEAR IN THAT CAVE!
©John L. Hart FLP
WITH A QUICK DAB OF HALLUCINOGENIC FROG JUICE...
RUB
HE SHOULD GO DOWN WITHOUT ANY TROUBLE.
FWOONK
OUCH!
OUCH?
DID EITHER OF YOU PENGUINS SEE WHICH WAY THAT PURPLE REFRIGERATOR WENT?
MASON
www.JohnHartStudios.com

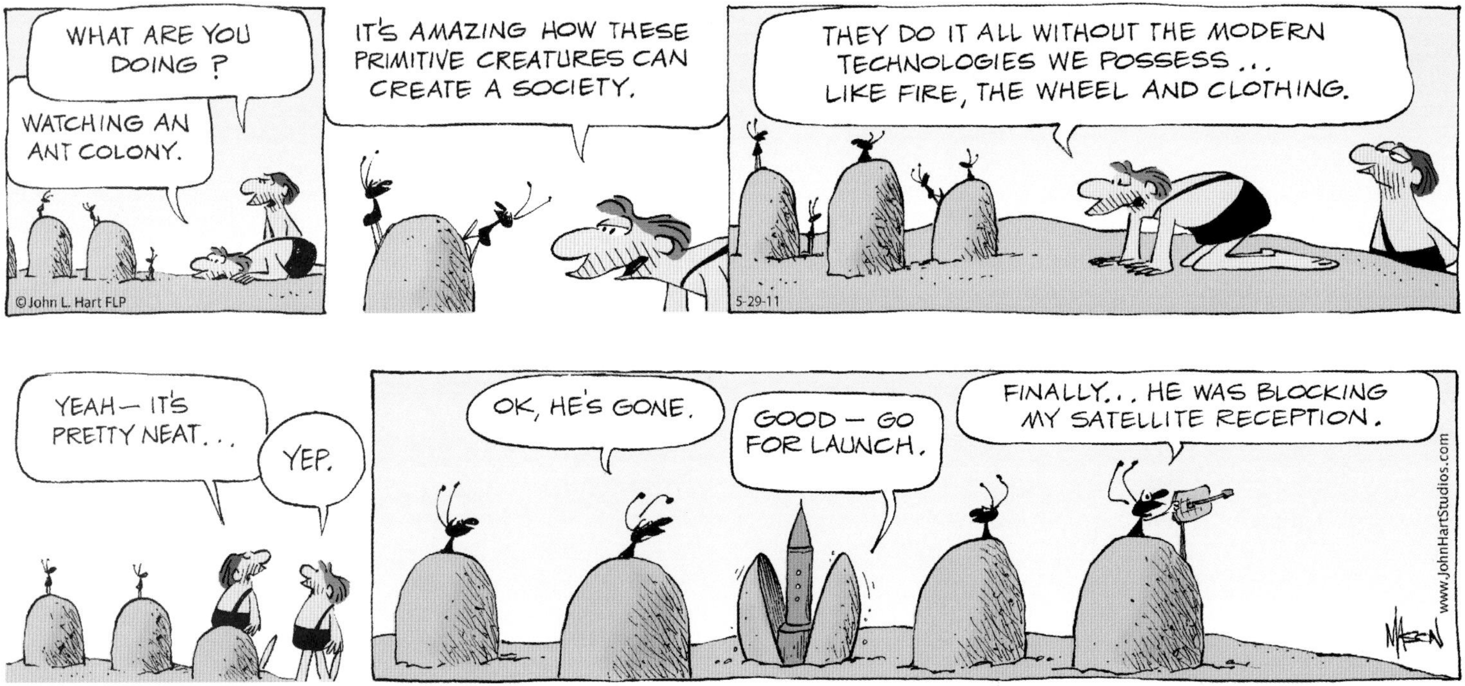
WHAT ARE YOU DOING ?
WATCHING AN ANT COLONY.
©John L. Hart FLP
IT'S AMAZING HOW THESE PRIMITIVE CREATURES CAN CREATE A SOCIETY.
THEY DO IT ALL WITHOUT THE MODERN TECHNOLOGIES WE POSSESS... LIKE FIRE, THE WHEEL AND CLOTHING.
5-29-11
YEAH— IT'S PRETTY NEAT...
YEP.
OK, HE'S GONE.
GOOD — GO FOR LAUNCH.
FINALLY... HE WAS BLOCKING MY SATELLITE RECEPTION.
www.JohnHartStudios.com

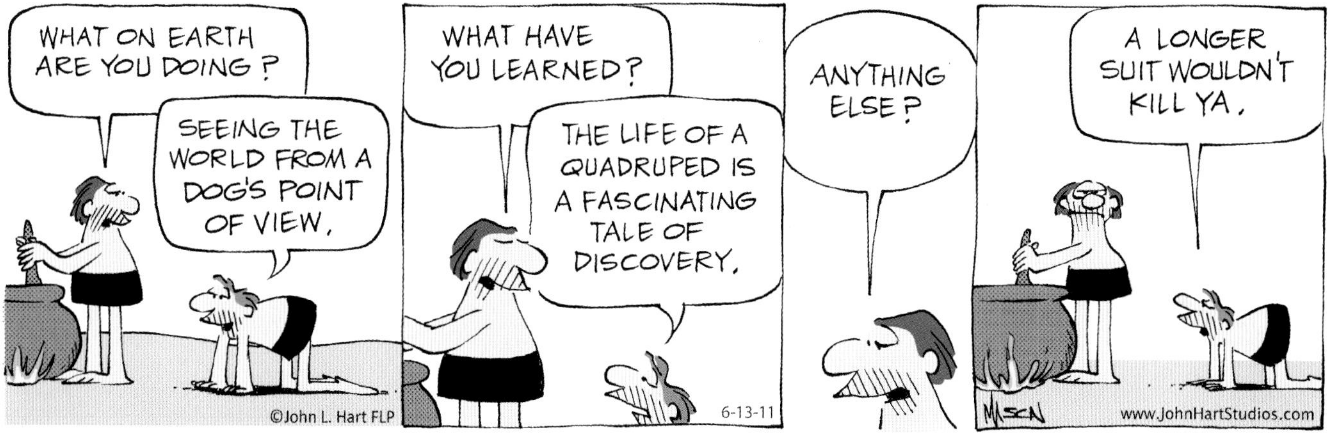
WHAT ON EARTH ARE YOU DOING?
SEEING THE WORLD FROM A DOG'S POINT OF VIEW.
WHAT HAVE YOU LEARNED?
THE LIFE OF A QUADRUPED IS A FASCINATING TALE OF DISCOVERY.
ANYTHING ELSE?
A LONGER SUIT WOULDN'T KILL YA.
©John L. Hart FLP
6-13-11
MASON
www.JohnHartStudios.com

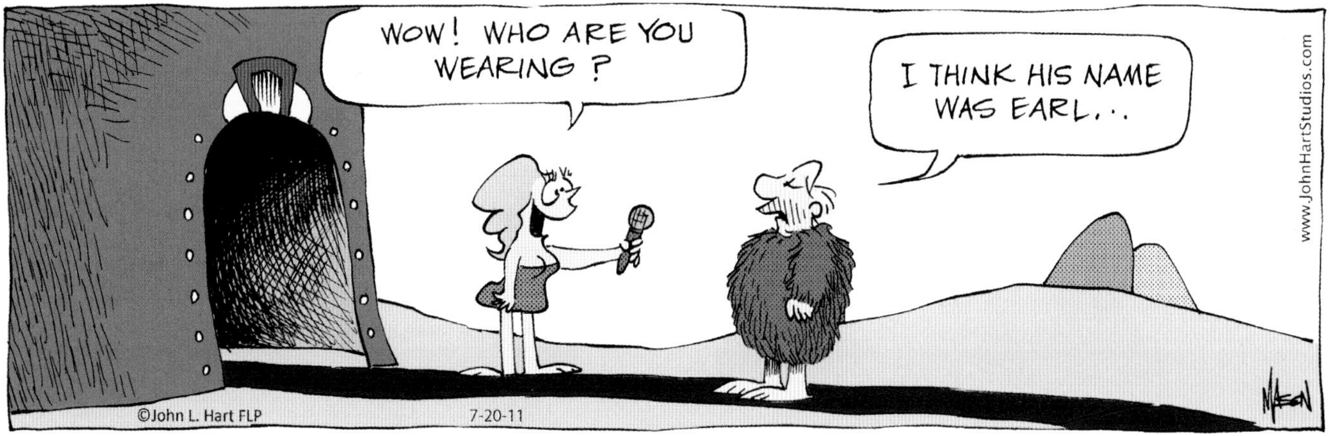
WOW! WHO ARE YOU WEARING?
I THINK HIS NAME WAS EARL...
www.JohnHartStudios.com
©John L. Hart FLP
7-20-11
MASON

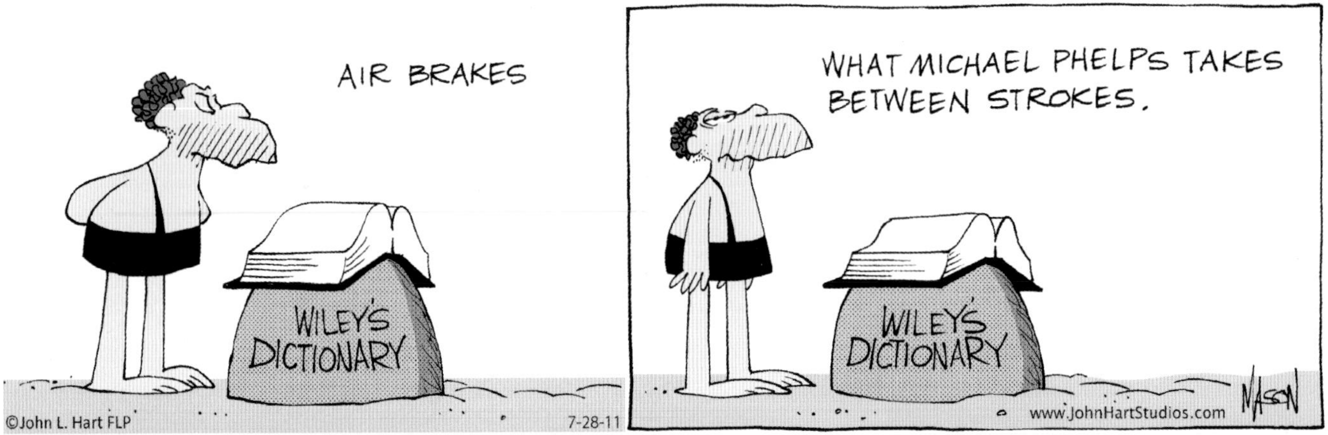
AIR BRAKES
WILEY'S DICTIONARY
©John L. Hart FLP
7-28-11
WHAT MICHAEL PHELPS TAKES BETWEEN STROKES.
WILEY'S DICTIONARY
www.JohnHartStudios.com
MASON

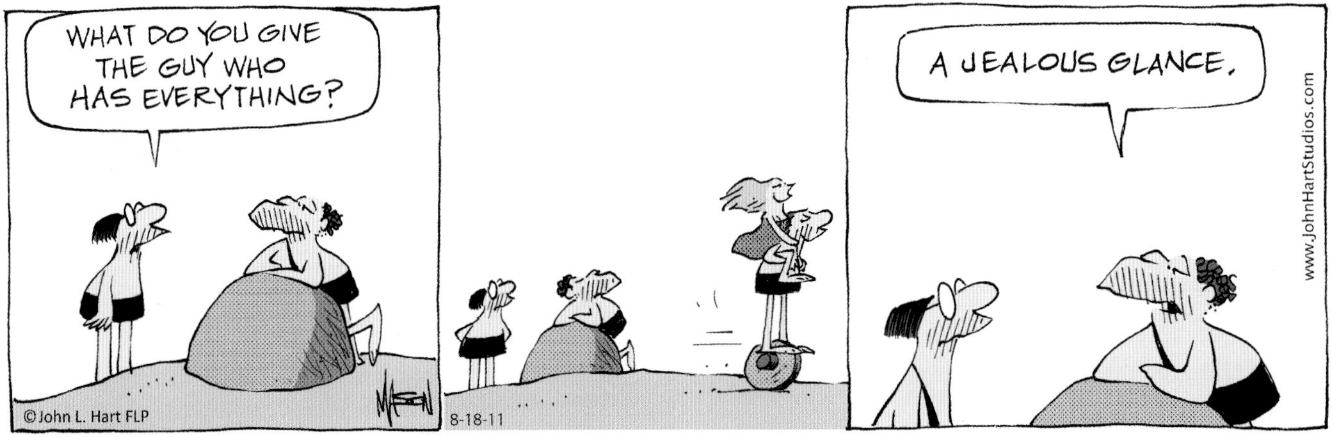
WHAT DO YOU GIVE THE GUY WHO HAS EVERYTHING?
©John L. Hart FLP
MASON
8-18-11
A JEALOUS GLANCE.
www.JohnHartStudios.com

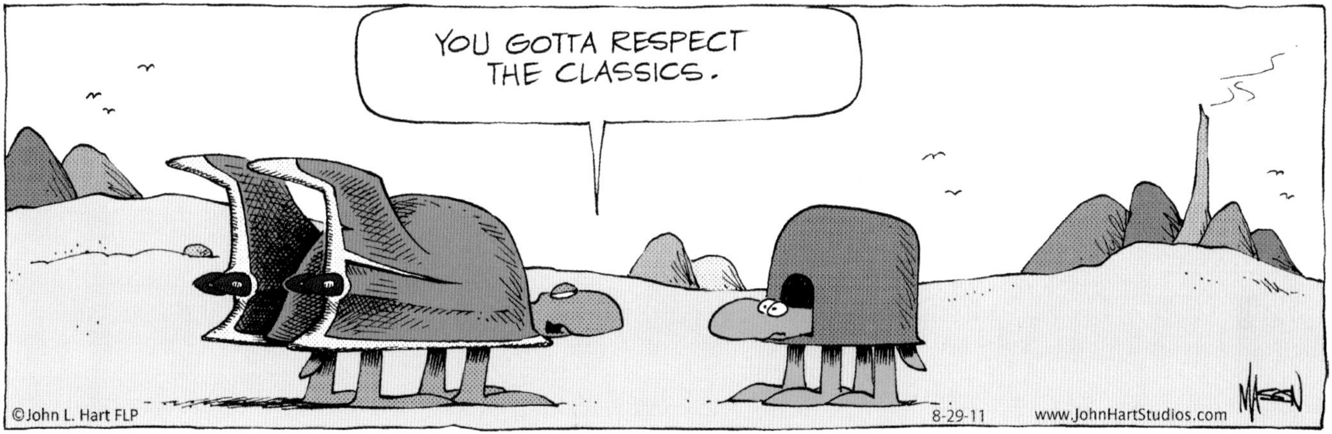
YOU GOTTA RESPECT THE CLASSICS.
©John L. Hart FLP
8-29-11
www.JohnHartStudios.com
MASON

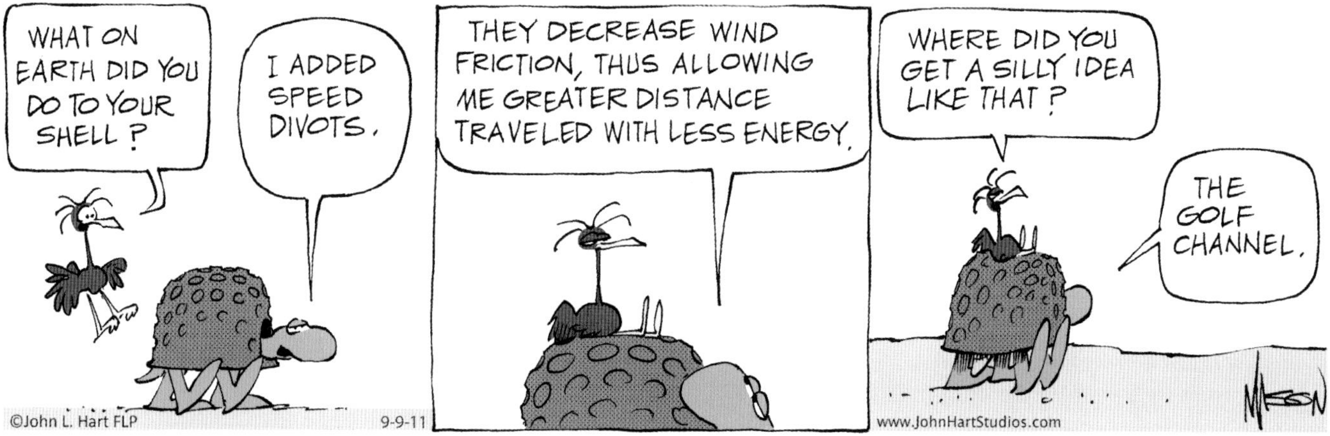
WHAT ON EARTH DID YOU DO TO YOUR SHELL ?
I ADDED SPEED DIVOTS.
THEY DECREASE WIND FRICTION, THUS ALLOWING ME GREATER DISTANCE TRAVELED WITH LESS ENERGY.
WHERE DID YOU GET A SILLY IDEA LIKE THAT ?
THE GOLF CHANNEL.
©John L. Hart FLP
9-9-11
www.JohnHartStudios.com
MASON

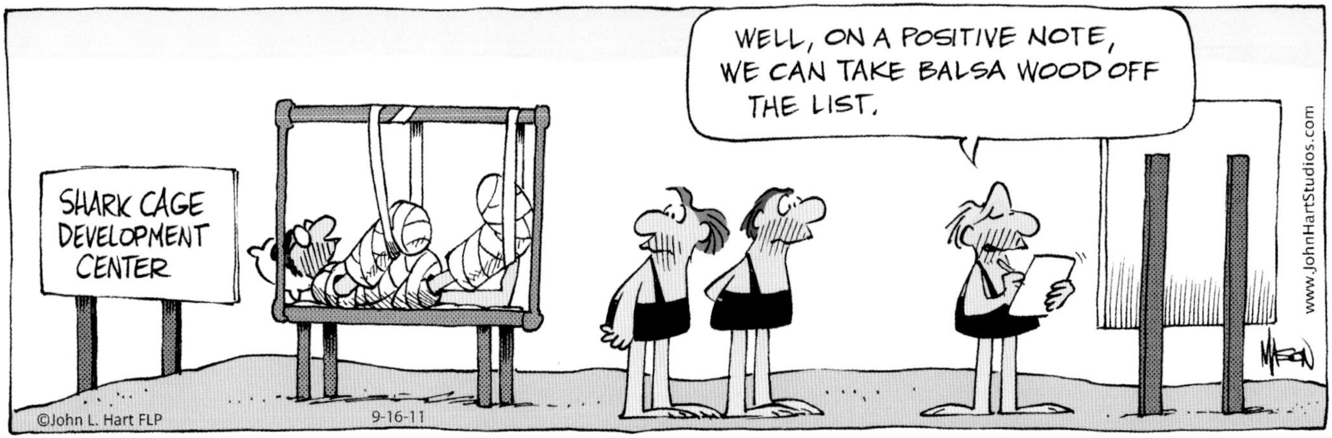
SHARK CAGE DEVELOPMENT CENTER
WELL, ON A POSITIVE NOTE, WE CAN TAKE BALSA WOOD OFF THE LIST.
©John L. Hart FLP
9-16-11
www.JohnHartStudios.com
MASON

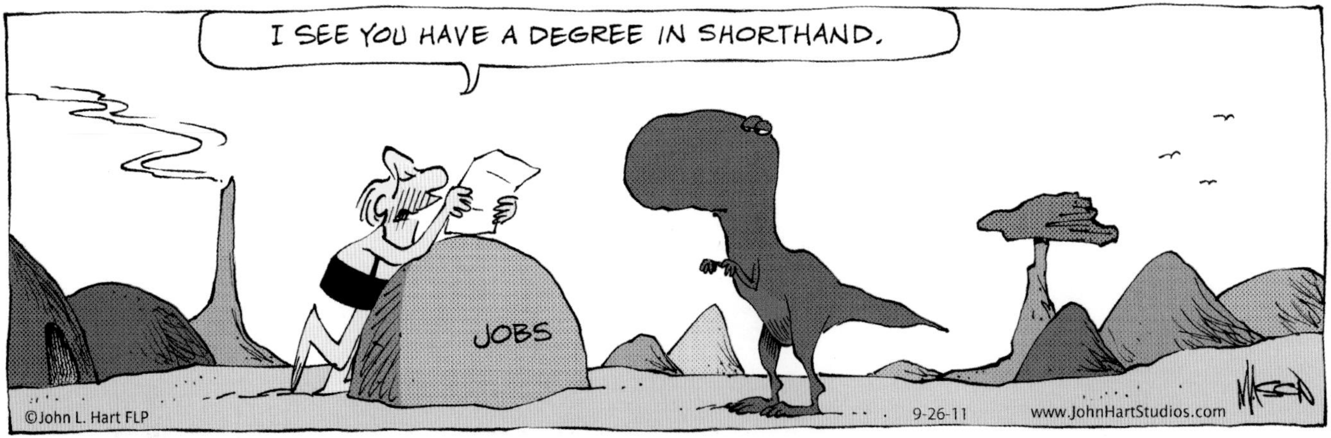
I SEE YOU HAVE A DEGREE IN SHORTHAND.
JOBS
©John L. Hart FLP
9-26-11
www.JohnHartStudios.com
MASON

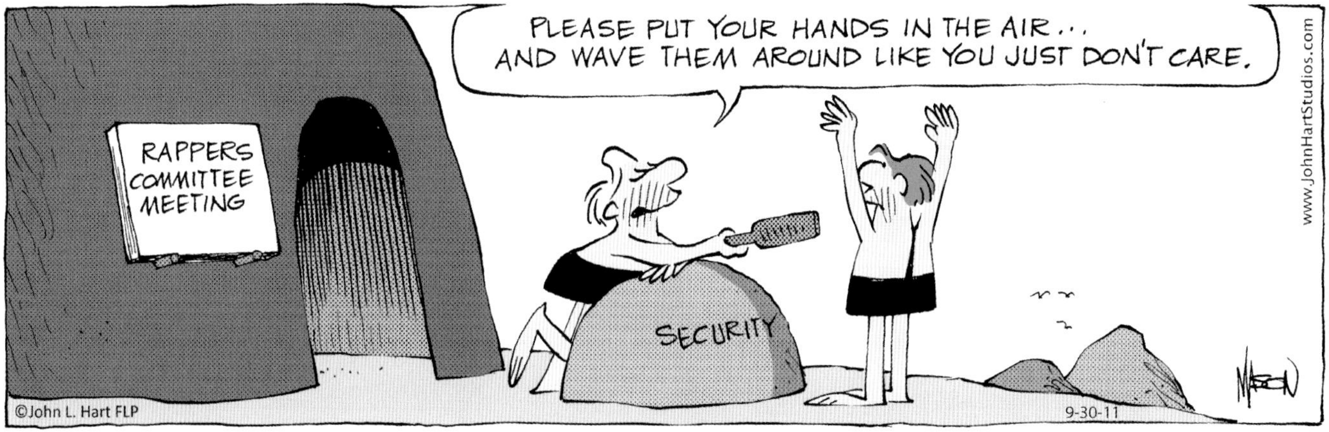
PLEASE PUT YOUR HANDS IN THE AIR...
AND WAVE THEM AROUND LIKE YOU JUST DON'T CARE.
RAPPERS COMMITTEE MEETING
SECURITY
www.JohnHartStudios.com
©John L. Hart FLP
9-30-11

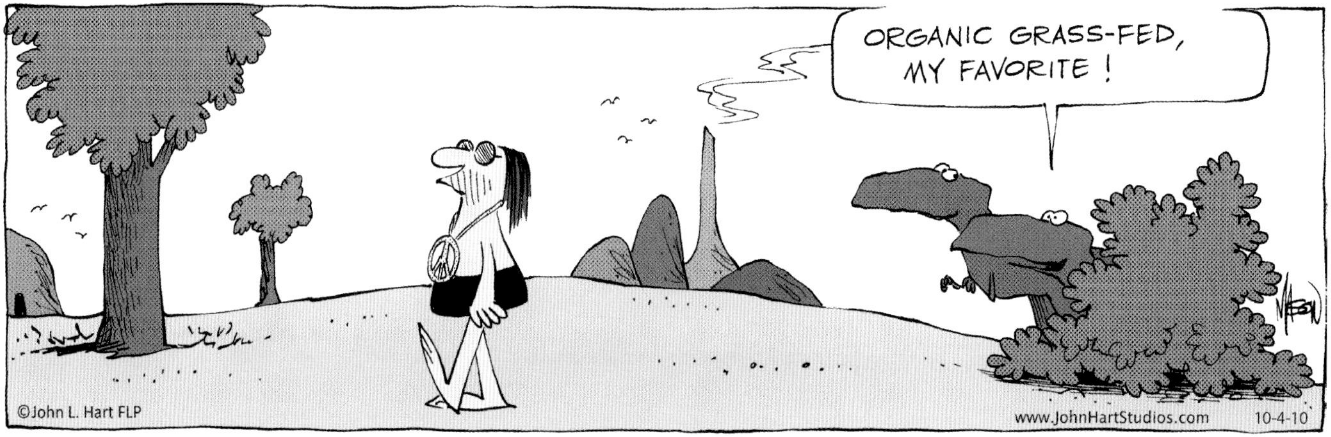
ORGANIC GRASS-FED,
MY FAVORITE !
©John L. Hart FLP
www.JohnHartStudios.com
10-4-10

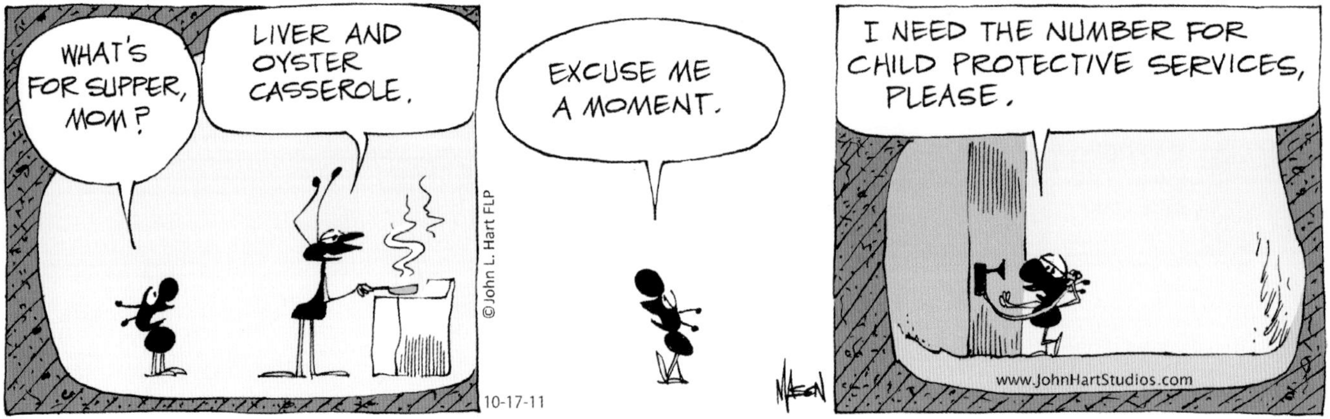
WHAT'S FOR SUPPER, MOM?
LIVER AND OYSTER CASSEROLE.
EXCUSE ME A MOMENT.
I NEED THE NUMBER FOR CHILD PROTECTIVE SERVICES, PLEASE.
©John L. Hart FLP
10-17-11
www.JohnHartStudios.com

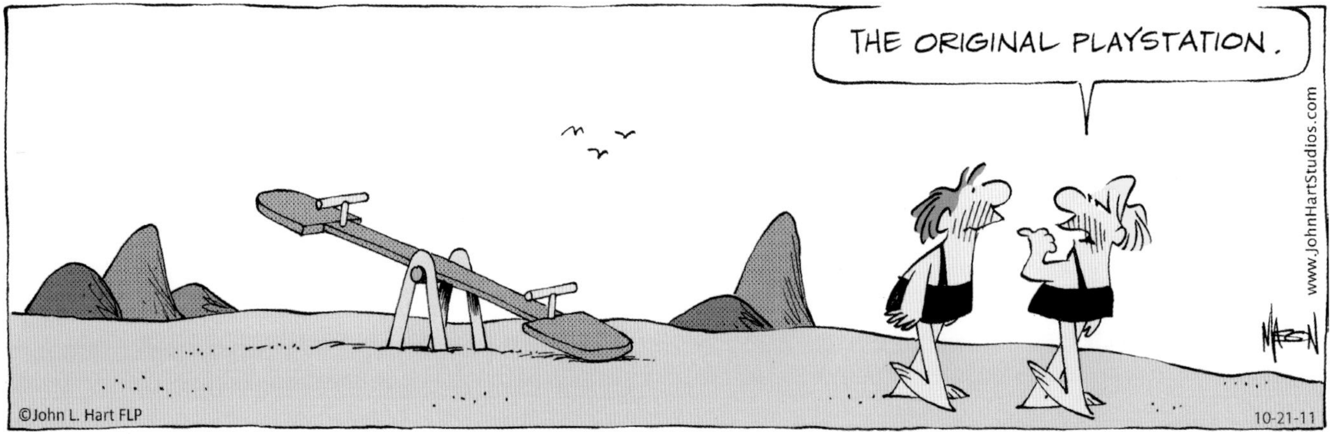
THE ORIGINAL PLAYSTATION.
www.JohnHartStudios.com
©John L. Hart FLP
10-21-11